12 Days Of Ghana

by

Dot Henderson

First published by AuthorHouse 11/09/04

ISBN: 1-4184-1382-8 (e-book)
ISBN: 1-4184-1381-X (Paperback)

Library of Congress Control Number: 2004090067

Printed in the United States of America
Bloomington, IN

This book is printed on acid free paper.

Dedication

Categorically, I dedicate this book:

To, the ladies of the tour group, Camille, Evelyn, Jessica, Lea, Lena, Lenora, Roberta, Sarah, Susan, and Thomasina. I offer special recognition to Lena and Lenora who planted the idea to take the trip.

To, my mom and dad, Samuel and Eloise Whitworth, I want to thank you for being supportive of me through the years. In addition, I want to make a special dedication to my daughter, Lavette, and my sisters, and brothers.

To my dearest, Ulysses, thank you so much for coming into my life at a time when I needed to advance to another level of existence. You have made such a difference in my life. You said that everyone should see Africa at least once. Thank you for making this trip possible.

To the rest of my African Family around the world and to all others who have an interest in knowing and witnessing the trails of injustice of Blacks during the years of slavery.

Acknowledgement

I wish to express my deepest appreciation to the following for bringing such life and meaning to the tours:

The Tour Guides with Land Tours of Ghana: Sly, Stephen, and Fred
The Tour Guide at Nkrumah Memorial
The Tour Guide at Dr. W.E.B. Du Bois Memorial Center
The Tour Guide at Cape Coast Castle
The Tour Guide at Elmina Castle
The Tour Guide at the King's Palace
The Tour Guide at Aburi Botanical Gardens

Table of Contents

Introduction

When making the decision to take this trip, I was just finishing up a challenging school year and needed a mental break. I needed time to just clear my head and think about anything but my most recent thoughts. I am not sure of the motivation, but I have always wanted to travel to Africa. My friends had approached me with the idea of taking the trip several months earlier. I had so much going on at school that I could not focus too much attention on the trip. I have learned to prioritize my thoughts and activities to avoid becoming overwhelmed.

Once school was out, I, then, had to complete the planning of my Family Reunion, which was scheduled for the 1st weekend in July. After the reunion, I began to think more seriously about the African Tour. The organizers never told me that I had missed the deadline for the trip, so I just proceeded with my planning and arrived in time to take the flight. I can only say that it must have been written in the cards to take this trip.

With each day's experience, as I traversed the country, I knew that it would be necessary to share this experience with the people back home. It became impossible not to associate, connect, or affiliate the pain and suffering felt there, with the pain and suffering felt back in the US. I returned home with a new perspective on life. The trip was a very spiritual, very cultural, and very humbling experience.

Each day of the tour, as we were leaving, one of the group members would lead us in prayer. I felt the entire trip was so spiritual that I wanted to include a daily reading from the Bible to coincide with the reading of this book. I selected the Book of Ecclesiastes. It has exactly twelve chapters and much of the reading is parallel to the events of this book which, I feel, will offer a better appreciation and understanding for this material.

Once back in the States, I was with one of my travel associates, waiting for my ride to return home. She did not now that I was watching, but as she moved about her home, she would pick up the smallest items and examine them as though she was seeing them for the first time. It was meditation in motion. I know what she was experiencing because I felt the same way. This trip transforms you. There is a new appreciation for what you have, and at the same time, you feel that you should have more and be doing more with your life. Many books have been written about the continent of Africa. This book is intended to refresh your interest for Africa. Hopefully, you will be inspired to go see for yourself. If you cannot go then, *read* again, about the Motherland.

Day I
Saturday 26-07-2003

All things are full of labour;
Man can not utter it; the eye is not satisfied with seeing,
Nor the ear filled with hearing.
The thing that hath been, it is that which shall be,
And that which is done is that which shall be done;
And there is no new thing under the sun.
Ecclesiastes 1:8-9

JFK (Ghana Airways Flight #151)

Journal Entry…

      The tour group arrived at JFK airport in New York at 1000 hours for a flight at 1300 hours to Ghana, Africa. We met at Ghana Airways, terminal 4. The all female members of the tour group included a business owner, a retired EEOC employee (I could have used her a few years ago), a nutritionist, a hospital human resource director and her daughter (who was about to enter college in the fall), and the rest of us were educators. A member of the travel agency from Ghana had traveled over to meet us. He greeted us and helped us get checked in. He, then, accompanied us on the return flight to Ghana.

1

We boarded the plane at 1230 hours, although the flight did not depart until 1500 hours. Ghana does not have its own airline crew; instead a flight crew is chartered out of Canada. The crew was predominately White and the flight instructions were given in English and French. As I looked around the plane of about 300 passengers, all of which were Black, I realized that I was in for a true cultural experience.

Point of Interest...
Pre-Colonial Period

Archaeological remains found in the coastal zone indicate that the area has been inhabited since the early "Bronze Age" (4000B.C.). Archaeological work suggest that central Ghana, north of the forest zone was inhabited as early as 3000 to 4000 years ago. There are other reports that the ancestors of some of Ghana's residents entered this area at least as early as the tenth century A.D. and that migration from the north and east continued thereafter.

These migrations resulted, in part, from the formation of a series of large states in the western Sudan. The northern area of Ghana was believed to have been ruled, initially, by nobles from Sudan. Trade from western Sudan established contacts with southern Ghana. The name Ghana was that of an Arab King, later capital and state.

Early rulers were renowned for their wealth in gold and their warrior hunting skills. They were also masters in gold trade. The valuable skills of goldsmiths came down from one generation to another for thousands of years. As far back as the Eighth Century, Ancient Ghana was known as "the land of gold" and described as one of the three most organized states in the region (the others being Gao and Kanem in the central Sudan).

Akan speaking people began to move in the forest region around the 15th century. With this migration, came new crops such as, bananas and cassava.

By the 17th century, the Ashante people, a branch of the Akan, began to expand in military forces in the central forest zone and an empire was formed making its capital in Kumasi.

Modern Day Ghana

The nation of Ghana is located in Western Africa. It has a population of 18.9m people, as of 2000, slightly smaller than the state of Oregon. It borders Burkina Faso to the north, Cote d"Ivoire to the west, Togo to the east, and the Atlantic Ocean to the south (Latitude: 5 degrees, 36 minutes north; Longitude: 0 degrees, 10 minutes east, a few degrees north of the equator).

In 1957, when it gained its independence, the new country was named after ancient Ghana. Although there are many ethnic groups, the Akans are recorded as the largest. This group is subdivided into groups such as the Bono, Ashante, Fanti and Sehwi. The most dominant language among the Akan is Twi and Fante. Twi (pronounced Chi) is predominant in the country and Fante is spoken in the coastal region. There are other dialects spoken in the Western Region of the country. However, English is the official language.

The climate is tropical. The average daily temperature is 30°C (86F) and the minimum temperature is around 23°C (76F). The eastern coastal belt is warm and comparatively dry; the southwest corner, hot and humid; and the north, hot and dry. There are two distinct rainy seasons in the south, May-June and August-September; in the north, the rainy seasons tend to merge. The coolest time of the year is between June and September. Annual rainfall in the coastal zone averages 83 centimeters (33 inches).

The manmade Volta Lake extends from the Akosombo Dam in southeastern Ghana to the town of Yapei, 520 kilometers (325 miles) to the north. The lake generates electricity, provides inland transportation, and is a potentially valuable resource for irrigation and fish farming. Today, there are 10 regions in Ghana, each with their own capital.

The following is an outline of the regions:

Regions	Capitals
Upper West Region	Wa
Upper East Region	Bolgatonga
Northern Region	Tamale
Brong Ahafo Region	Suyani
Volta Region	Ho
Ashanti Region	Kumasi
Central Region	Cape Coast
Eastern Region	Koforidua
Western Region	Sekondi
Greater Accra Region	Accra

More on the regions later...

Economy

Ghana is a low-income country. Thirty-two percent of the population is below poverty level. Agriculture equates to 36% of the Gross National Product (GNP), industry equates to 25% and services equate to 39%.

Inflation Rate   **Unemployment Rate =20.3 (2001)**

30% (April 2003)
29.6% (June 2003)   **Minimum Wage** = 9200 Cedis as of 01-02-03
27.7 (August 2003)

The Labor Force by Occupation

Agriculture/ 60%   **Industry/** 15%   **Services/** 25%

Health

The average life expectancy for males is 55.66 years and 57.43 years for females. 170,000 children have been orphaned because they parents have died from Aids. Another 173,000 children are identified at risk of being infected. As of 2001, 360,000 people are living with Aids. The health care system is cash and carry; however, the government is working to implement a full-scale health insurance plan.

4

Religion

Earlier reports show 62% of the people are of Christian faith (including Catholics, Methodists, Presbyterian, Pentecostal) and are predominately in the central and southern regions. The Muslims are concentrated in the north and represent about 15% of the people. The remaining 22% include indigenous or non-believers.

Holidays

6th March	Independence Day
	Good Friday
	Easter
1st May	May Day
1st July	Republic Day
1st August	Emancipation Day
25th December	Christmas

Transportation

The cars are mostly compact, Toyotas, Volkswagons, Renaults, BMWs, and Mercedes. The guide said there were 3 limousines at one time but they were eventually replaced. They don't seem to fit into this society. There is a railroad system that serves mostly southern industrial areas such as Accra and Kumasi. There are 11 domestic airfields including Kotoka International. Major ports include Tema and Lake Volta.

Industry

The primary industry includes mining gold, and magnesium. Cocoa, gold, and timber are among the foreign trade to the U.S., Japan, Germany, and Britain. Major crops are yams, corn, cassava, and root crops.

Journal Entry...

After about one hour in flight, dinner was served. The menu consisted of a choice of chicken or lamb, with a vegetable medley and rice. A small square cake and drinks were also served. This was an 11-hour flight. We stopped in Portugal, Spain around the 7th hour to refuel. This stop took about an hour but we did not depart the plane. Once we were in the air again, we were served breakfast and watched an in-flight movie "How to lose a guy in two weeks." Breakfast consisted of Danish, a croissant, a fruit cup and juice. Around 0500 hours, we began to fly out of the darkness into the light. We arrived in Accra, Ghana at 0600 hours Sunday morning, 27 July. Ghana time is 4 hours ahead of Eastern Standard Time, so it was 0200 hours at home.

Day II
Sunday 27-07-2003

There is nothing better for a man;
than that he should eat and drink,
And that he should make his soul enjoy good in his labour.
This also I saw, that it was from the hand of God.
Ecclesiastes 2:24

Kotoka International Airport

Journal Entry...

Getting through Customs was not difficult. We completed an immigration form on the plane requesting name, home address, and address in Ghana where we would be staying. Once off the plane, we handed the form and our passport to a lady behind a window. She verified the information and stamped the passport. From there, we proceeded to pick up our luggage. The group had placed identical ribbons on our entire luggage before checking them at JFK. This made it easier to locate at baggage claim, especially since one piece of luggage was placed in another pile.

0800 hours, we are ready for the once in a lifetime experience that awaits us. Moving through the crowd, we saw someone holding up a sign with our group leader's name. His shirt matched the shirt of the guide that met us in New York, so we knew he was our guide. He directed us to the tourbus. By the way, there were several tours in town from the US, groups from New York and Atlanta.

Golden Tulip Hotel

Riding through the city, the sites around town immediately dispelled those preconceived notions that Africa was all tribal, fighting, and poverty. There are Internet cafes on every block. Accra is a thriving city just as any city in the US. As the tour bus pulled into the entrance of the Golden Tulip Hotel where we were staying, African Dancers, wearing very colorful prints and performing cultural dance steps, greeted us. It was wonderful! Once out of the tour bus, the travel agent and Co-owner officially greeted us and led us to a conference room inside the hotel for briefing. We were served refreshments, given our room keys and accommodation instructions, and briefed on do's and don'ts (such as don't drink the water because it could cause dysentery). It was recommended to use bottled water, even when brushing our teeth. We were assigned two tour-guides and the driver for our group.

After we checked into our rooms and had an opportunity to view the hotel, we all agreed that it was about the equivalent of a Marriott in the states. We had been informed to remember that we were away from home and hotel accommodations may not be the same, but we were certainly off to a good start. When I turned on the TV in the room, there was a video channel with Black music from the US. Looking around a hotel of this caliber and seeing all Blacks running the operation was a sight to behold. The service was superb!

There was a business center in the hotel with about 10 computers, and fax machines. I would be able to e-mail my family back home to inform them that I had arrived safe and sound. There was a nightclub, a patio bar at the pool, and a great dining room. There was a casino down stairs, a gift shop and a clothing store. The Annafi Forex Bureau was also on site to convert American dollars to Ghanaian Cedis (pronounced CD's). I paid 2000 Cedis per minute to e-mail back home.

Kokrobite Beach

After lunch and a brief respite, we traveled about 15 miles to Kokrobite Beach for a colorful welcoming performance by the dancers of the African Arts and Music Academy. The facility was located right along the Atlantic Ocean. There was no beach, just the ocean as a backdrop. We sat and watched the performance as the cool ocean breeze satisfied our thirst for air-conditioning.

Along the road to the beach, we had an opportunity to see the depressed area outside Accra. There were small villages of people. Some lived in houses made of mud. Some had outdoor community shower stalls. I noticed this when I saw someone go inside what I had seen, perhaps on the TV series "Mash." There was no roof and I could see the showerhead in the stall. I was told many of these people did not have indoor plumbing and something was rigged up outside that could be used by the neighbors.

I saw numerous goats and sheep that walked the streets as dogs do in the states. I asked about the possibility of theft and was told by the guide that very little theft of a person's goats and sheep occurs. There were people outside preparing foods. For instance, I saw a lady stirring what appeared to be a large bowl of batter for bread. There were people cooking over make shift grills. In many instances, these meals were being prepared for sale to the neighbors. One person had bread to sell, another person had meats. Although what I saw appeared to be poverty, there was great entrepreneurship going on here with plenty of supply and demand. It was heart warming to see my Brothers and Sisters making life work for them.

There is no welfare system. I saw many cinder block foundations for housing construction. The guide said that because of their financial status, the people were unable to finance, many would take up to 10 years to build a house. As they obtain money for supplies, they would build, but then some never complete the construction. I was also told that no one owns the land in Ghana. There is a leasehold agreement. The Ghanaians can hold the land for 75 years and Non-Ghanaians can hold the land for 50 years.

At 1700 hours, we headed back to the Golden Tulip Hotel to prepare for dinner at 1900 hours. Our group had a reserved table. The dinner was buffet and the presentations were great, from salads to rice and pasta, and from chicken to fish, roast beef and turkey and several delicious desserts. The food was great, but a little more spice than I was accustomed to. After dinner, some of the group turned in early because tomorrow was going to be a busy day. Others sat on the patio to listen to the cultural music.

Day III
Monday 28-07-2003

To everything there is a season, and a time to
every purpose under the heaven;
a time to be born, and a time to die; a time to plant and a time to pluck
up that which is planted; a time to kill, and a time to heal;
a time to break down, and a time to build up;
a time to weep, and a time to laugh; a time to mourn, and a time to
dance, a time to cast away stones, and a time to gather stones together;
a time to embrace, and a time to refrain from embracing; a time to get,
and a time to lose; a time to keep, and a time to cast away; a time to
rend, and a time to sew, a time to keep silence, and a time to speak; a
time to love, and a time to hate; a time of war, and a time of peace.
Ecclesiastes 3:1-8

Accra

Journal Entry...

We had breakfast in the hotel. Two meals per day were included in the package (breakfast and dinner). We needed to convert money so we went to the Annafi Forex Bureau there in the hotel. The women were ecstatic to be carrying around $1 million. One hundred twenty American dollars is equal to $1,032,000 Cedis. With cash in hand, we were ready to take on the City of Accra. Accra has been the administrative and economic capital of Ghana since 1876 when its capital was moved from Cape Coast in the Central region. It is a 125-year old city that has a blend of colonial and modern architecture. It has a population of 2.5m people.

We met the tour guides at 0845 hours to formally tour the city of Accra. We saw the neighborhoods, lower, middle, and upper class. Many of the residents in the middle and upper neighborhoods are called been-to's (they have been to other lands, acquired skills and money and now have returned home). We also saw the commercial and governmental district including the U.S. Embassy, State House and police department. No pictures are allowed of the police or military. The guide stated that if we were caught taking pictures, we would be chased and our film would be destroyed. Luckily, we did not see any military or policemen.

There were people all over the streets, selling items. Most were young people, males and females. They are called street hawkers. Many of them had trays

10

balanced on their heads. They sold bags of water, flags, maps, candy, gum, and clothes. You name it! They were selling it. It was amazing, to say the least. There were also women carrying their babies on their backs, methodically wrapped and totally supported in fabric. I thought maybe there was some type of tow beneath the fabric, as we use in the states, until I saw a lady actually wrap her child in the fabric. It was quite an undertaking.

Point of Interest...
Story of Cocoa

There is an interesting story about Cocoa, first brought to Ghana by Teteh Quashie, around 1878. He was working as a pawn slave in Fenandepo, an island on the West Coast of Africa. When he was freed, he swallowed the cocoa seedlings and upon returning to Ghana, the seedlings passed through his digestive system. He planted the seedlings and they flourished. The farmers accepted the challenge and also got some of the seedlings from the first cocoa tree, planted them and by doing so, cocoa became the chief export. There is an area downtown called Cocoa Circle in honor of the former slave.

The Memorial of Dr. Kwame Nkrumah
Journal Entry...

We met the curator to tour the Memorial of Dr. Kwame Nkrumah, the 1ˢᵗ President of Ghana. Dr. Nkrumah was part of the UGCC (United Gold Coast Convention) of Ghana in 1947. In 1949, he formed the CPP (Convention People's Party). This led to 3 years of imprisonment.

Although, he did emerge through his party to declare Ghana the 1ˢᵗ independent African nation south of the Sahara Desert. Dr. Nkrumah died 27-04-72. This memorial became his 3ʳᵈ and final resting-place in 1992. It is a dynamic display of art and water. I learned that everything has a meaning.

There are 7 sculptured men with horns in a pool of water. Seven represents 7 days of creation and the water represents life. The total meaning, "The Creator always lives. If God dies, I also die." The nation's flag also flies overhead. It is green, red, and yellow with a black star in the center of the flag. The green stands for forests and vegetation. The red stands for the blood of the people. The yellow stands for the minerals, and of course, the black stands for the people.

The entrance into the mausoleum has a sculptured wall. A man leads the left side with a sword that symbolizes authority. A woman leads the right side with a staff holding an egg, which symbolizes balance. Combine the 2 to mean a balance of authority in power. Directly over the entrance is a sculpture of a large eagle with 3 heads carved within its body. This means 3 heads are better than one. There is strength in unity. We also visited the village of Jamestown where Dr. Nkrumah was imprisoned at the James Fort Prison for 3 years. The people, indigenous to this area, are called "the Gas People." This is the oldest area in Accra.

1200 hours, it was lunchtime. The guides took us to the Country Kitchen Restaurant. Because of a sensitive stomach in the states, I had purchased lunch items before leaving home and packaged things such as tuna and peanut butter and crackers among my luggage. So, rather than explore just yet, I had taken my tuna with me for the tour today. I did order pineapple that is plentiful in this area and good! Some of the other members of the tour ordered Kentucky Fried Chicken and chips from the menu. Okay, not the colonel's, but I was told that it was a tasty dish.

Dr. W.E.B. Du Bois Center for Pan African Culture

After lunch, we were off to the W.E.B. Du Bois Center for Pan African Culture. Dr. Du Bois was a Civil Rights Activist and author who championed the civil rights of people of color all over the world. He had an integral and controversial role in improving the humanitarian rights of Blacks and the establishment of the NAACP. He was founder of the NAACP's "Crisis Magazine." He conducted studies on the problems affecting Blacks in America that drew criticism from both Blacks and Whites. The Whites felt "why study the obvious," and the Blacks felt they were likened to test animals.

In 1961, at the age of 93, Dr. Du Bois was invited to Ghana by President Nkrumah to assume directorship of The Encyclopedia Africana. This encyclopedia would be a compilation of research on Africa and its surrounding islands, in relation to the people and their lives, their history from pre-historic to current times, and their political, economic and social developments. Dr. Du Bois was not able to complete the project, he felt that the project should be a continuing effort which would grow and expand in the coming years.

Upon Dr. Du Bois' death, the project was reassigned, updated, and edited to produce three volumes. These volumes are the Dictionaries of African Biographies. Volume I covers Ghana and Ethiopia, published in 1977. Volume II covers Sierra Leone and Zaire, published in 1979. Volume III covers South Africa, Botswana, Lesotho, and Swaziland. Work is being done to produce the Volume IV that would cover Egypt and Nigeria.

When Dr. Du Bois left for Africa, he knew that he would not be returning to the states, so he took everything he owned with him. Among the Doctor's personal effects were his regalias from Fisk University (graduated with a B.A. in Philosophy and Social Sciences), Harvard University (graduated with a B.A. in Philosophy, Economics and History, a Master's Degree and a Ph.D. in History and Government), and Berlin University (Honorary Doctorate Degree). He had a library of over 1300 books. One, of which, "The Souls of Black Folk," he wrote in 1902. Dr. Du Bois is credited with many other literary works including poetry.

Point of Interest...

The following is an excerpt from the poem **"Children of the Moon:"**
I saw the black men huddle, Fumed in fear, falling face downward;
Vainly I clutched and clawed, Dumbly they cringed and cowered,
Moaning in mournful monotone, O Freedom, O Freedom, O Freedom,
over me, Before I'll be a slave, I'll be buried in my grave,
And go home to my God, and be free.

There is a picture of Dr. Du Bois at the center with the following inscription,

"One thing alone, I charge you as you live, believe in life! Always human beings will live and progress to greater, broader, and fuller life. The only possible death is to lose belief in the truth. Simply because the great end comes slowly because time is long." Last statement to the world, 1963

Dr. Du Bois died 27-08-63, one day before The March on Washington. He is memorialized at the home in which he lived. This is now The Center for Pan African Culture. Dr. Du Bois was married twice. He shared 53 years of marriage with his first wife, Nina Gomer. They had one child, Yolanda, who died suddenly at the age of 60, three years prior to his death. At the time of his death, he had been married to Shirley Graham for 12 years. When she died, she was cremated and placed in an urn beside him on site at the center.

Centre for National Culture
(The Greater Accra Region)
Journal Entry...

Now, it's time to spend some money. Off to the markets. The Center for National Culture is an outdoor textile market with everything for sale from clothes to fabrics, to handbags to hats and beads. The vendors are very aggressive. Everyone is selling something and they want you to buy their goods. In fact, they are willing to barter to make a sell. Aggressive is the operative word to describe the vendors. It's around 1800 hours and time to go back to the hotel to prepare for dinner. What a day! Oh, but the day was not over. There were vendors who came to the hotel with wears and art for sale. The skills of the vendors are so incredible. The ladies can make dresses and the men can carve and paint the art and weave material. It is mind boggling to see such talents. We must find a way to expose more of these artists.

Day IV
Tuesday 29-07-03

So I returned, and considered all the
oppressions that are done under the sun;
And behold the tears of such as were
oppressed, and they had no comforter;
And on the side of their oppressors there was
power; but they had no comforter.
Ecclesiastes 4:1

Elmina Beach Resort Hotel

Journal Entry...
    We were late leaving this morning. The tour guides had the challenge of securing our luggage on top of the bus. By the time we checked out of the Golden Tulip, it was around 0900 hours. We were headed for the Cape Coast, called the Fante land and the people are the Fanti. It was a bumpy ride all the way. There were potholes, as bad as the ones in the states after a bad winter. The driver missed a lot of them, but not all of them. As we traveled the country roads, we saw ant castles 11-12 ft tall. The area enroute was not very populated. There was an occasional community. I kept looking for farmland.

15

This area seemed perfect for crops. There was a lot of vegetation. If it were groomed and pruned, it would be very appealing. I had fallen asleep and when I awoke, the others talked about seeing a monkey hanging from a tree by the tail. It was probably dead and would be eaten by other animals.

We arrived at the Elmina Beach Resort around 1130 hours. This is a lovely hotel, positioned along the coastline of the Atlantic Ocean. The layout of this resort is quite unique. There is the main facility for check in, conferences, and meals. Then, you exit that building to go to the rooms, some of which are suites. There is a tennis court, a basketball court, and an exercise room. There was also a business center with computers to e-mail back home. I paid 1000 Cedis per minute to e-mail back home.

We had lunch at the hotel. Our room faced the ocean. My roommate and I sat on the veranda and ate Tuna and crackers. We must have sat there for an hour. It started to get cold, so we got up to go back inside. As we entered the room, having left the patio door open, moisture from the ocean had settled on the floor and we had to have the maid service mop up the puddle of water.

We met the group in the lobby and headed off to the shopping mall around 1530 hours. Actually, this was an outdoor market. This market coincides with The PANAFEST & Emancipation 2003, which runs from 23-07-03 through 07-08-03. The PANAFEST (Pan African Festival) began in 1999 and is held every 2 years.

The theme for the 10-day festival is:
"The re-emergence of African civilization; uniting the African family," with a sub-theme "dialogue on traditional African system in 21st Century globalization." We are referred to as living in Diaspora, Blacks outside of Africa. There is a conference of African Traditional Leaders (ATL) who are partners in the development of Africa and the realization of the goals of the African union. The venue of activities took place in Accra, Cape Coast, Elmina, Assin Manso, Kumasi, and Satago.

A news article dated 29th July, 2003, quoted Jake Obetsebi-Lamptey, Ghana's Minister of Tourism, "African intellectuals owe it a duty to support the political leadership to move the New Partnership for Africa's Development (NEPAD), "from the bookshelves to reality." According to him, NEPAD is an African initiative, which shows African leaders, resolve to accept responsibility for the continent's problems and take its development into their own hands.

16

The shopping mall consisted of vendors who have come from neighboring towns to exhibit and sell their clothes and art. I cannot emphasize enough the quality of work and the preparation that has taken place here by these vendors. They paid for booths and have numerous items waiting to be sold.

There are also festivities at night including music and plenty of food. We did not attend any of those activities. The ladies in my group shopped until they dropped. They bought nice African attire and art carvings. Around 1700 hours, we headed back to the hotel. We had dinner on the outdoor patio. The meal was great. There were yams that looked like white potatoes and they were delicious. There were salads, cabbage, rice, pasta, fish, and chicken. After dinner, we met in our group leader's suite. Some of the ladies attempted to play a game without a clear understanding of the rules. It was funny watching them randomly drop, what appeared to be, rocks in a wood carved container without any rhyme or reason for doing so.

Later, as we headed back to our rooms, some of the young people, who had come over from Atlanta, GA for a youth conference, were playing basketball. That night, the waves beat so rough against the ocean's shore, it sounded as though the hotel would be washed away by morning.

Day V
Wednesday 30-07-03

Keep thy foot when thou goest to the house of God,
And be more ready to hear, than to give the sacrifice of fools; for they
consider not that they do evil. Be not rash with thy mouth, and let
not thine heart be hasty to utter any thing before God; for God is in
Heaven and thou upon earth; therefore let thy words be few.
Ecclesiastes 5:1-2

Kakum National Park

Journal Entry...

  Around 1000 hours, we traveled to Kakum National Park. This is a beautiful rainforest, the only one of its kind in Africa and one of four in the world. It is located in the Central Region of Ghana, about 20 kilometers north of Cape Coast. It covers 360 square kilometers of Ghana's rapidly dwindling rainforest. Kakum National Park was originally established in 1932, but was officially opened by the government in 1994. The rainforest is disappearing due to timber extraction and growing settlements. To combat the loss of the rainforest, a canopy walkway was built, offering a unique way to experience the rainforest.

18

We followed the park ranger on the trail up to the canopy walkway. Along the way there were signs that said, "quiet please, you are in someone else's home." So we had to proceed with little disturbances. The guide advised us that most of the animals sleep during the day and come out at night. They could see us but we probably could not see them. Long pants are recommended for the walk. A couple of us were wearing shorts.

The wildlife reserve is known to include the forest elephant, the Diana Monkey, the royal antelope, about 100 species of mammals, reptiles and amphibians, about 550 species of butterflies, as well as 250 species of birds including the Frazier-Eagle Owl, the African Grey and Senegal parrots, and much more.

This is such a thick, beautiful forest. The guide explained the cultural, economic, medicinal, and practical uses of the more than 40 forest plant species as we walked the trail. He pointed out the plant that Tarzan, from the movies, would swing from as he moved about the jungle. This plant grows independent of any other plants from the ground up. Then the guide climbed up the plant about 10 feet off the ground to show us the strength of it.

There was about a 20-minute walk up hill to the canopy. The walkway stands 100 feet above the forest. The canopy has a wood base with cable side rail suspensions. There are 7 sectional walkways, composed of 1000 feet of swinging bridge, attached to 6 tree-ports for breaks in case you lose you nerve along the way. The walkway was designed to depend upon trees for support, no nails or bolts were used. Instead, steel cables were carefully wrapped around trunks to provide stabilization. Only China, Malaysia, and Peru have similar walkways. Most of my group walked over and there was another group waiting to take on the challenge after us. I was hesitant to walk, initially, but once I got started, it was just another fear that I had overcome. I am glad that I did not miss the opportunity to walk so high above this beautiful forest. The view was breathtaking. I prayed as I walked and thanked God for the opportunity to just "be me."

Each person walking over was given a head start and we were to allow the one ahead of us to complete each section before we started. Being the last in my group, I started over and then felt an imbalance. I looked back and saw that a member of the next tour group was beginning to walk over. She was coming at such a fast pace that she would pass me. This created a problem, considering that the walkway was designed for one person at a time. I picked up my steps and got off the walkway. I met the rest of the group; we tipped the tour guide and left for lunch.

We had reserved lunch earlier at Hans Cottage Botel so that it would be ready when we got back. This was an interesting location. It was a motel with an outdoor café. There was a walkway over a pool of crocodiles that led to the seating area. The ladies seemed to like the chicken and chips. I, of course, had my tuna. After lunch, some of the ladies threw their leftovers into the water to see if there really were crocodiles. Yes! There were real crocodiles, a lot of them.

After lunch, we went back to the shopping mall. Again, the ladies shopped until they dropped or needed to convert more money. So, we had to find a Forex Bureau to make another conversion. On today, we found out that traveler's checks convert at a lower rate that U.S. dollars. So, next trip over, we will have to keep that in mind. The ladies also bought elephant oil, which I am told is good for what ails you. I did not buy any. I told them that I do plan to come back to Africa some day and If I have something that ails me at that time, then I would buy the oil.

Almost anywhere you travel, you will see some reference to God. There are clothing stores called "God's Heavenly Fashions" or "God is Able Fashions." Cars will have signs on the back that say "God is real" or "God is love." To see some areas depressed and other areas thriving, to see God's presence, and to see the beautiful people, all combined was an experience much unlike what is depicted by the media.

Around 1830 hours, we decided to attend a play and have a late dinner. The play was entitled "Ancestor's Vision" and sponsored by the government in conjunction with the PANAFEST. The theme of the play was related to the nobility rights of a young girl. As part of an old African custom, once young girls reach puberty, there is a ceremony giving them nobility rights. The young girl in the play was pregnant and needed to break the news to her mother that she was not deserving of this ceremony.

Even today, when a young girl becomes pregnant, she will attempt to keep this from her parents or her parents will avoid publicizing the daughter's situation. In this portrayal, the daughter commits suicide to prevent telling her mother. One of the performers wrote the play and it was performed at the arts center. It was very realistic and emotional. The play was over around 2030 hours and we went back to the hotel for dinner. Dinner looked familiar. It was a long day, after dinner we all retired for the evening. Later I washed some of my garments. I had purchased a liquid fruity body wash before leaving the states that I could also use for washing. The thoughts of traveling for 12 days without doing laundry was inconceivable.

Day VI
Thursday 31-07-03

There is an evil which I have seen under the sun, and it is common among men;
A man in which God hath given riches, wealth, and honour;
So that he wanteth nothing for his soul of all he that he desireth,
Yet God giveth him not power to eat thereof, but a stranger eateth it:
this is vanity, And it is an evil disease.
Ecclesiastes 6:1-2

Cape Coast Castle

Journal Entry...
    We slept later today and the tour guides picked us up around 0900 hours. Today's itinerary was to tour Cape Coast Castle and the Elmina Castle. This was about a 20-minute drive from the hotel. The weather is very pleasant today, as it has been on previous days. The mornings are cool and a little overcast. It starts to warm by noon. The average temperature is around 32°C. Sunset is around 1900 hours and then it cools off again. I have not yet experienced any mosquito bites.

21

The Forte of Cape Coast Castle

Cape Coast, the capital of the Central Region, is one of the most historic cities in Ghana. It was the center of the British Administration and capital of the Gold Coast by 1700 until 1877 when the capital moved to Accra. The people are called the Fanti and the language is Fante. Some say most of the oldest and best schools in Ghana are in Cape Coast. As we approached Cape Coast, the storefront buildings had an architectural influence of colonial times. The streets were filled with people.

We got off the bus and walked up to this door that opened up to the courtyard of a forte. Actually, this forte was called Cape Coast Castle and it backed up to the Atlantic Ocean, which was not noticeable from the street. There were cannons facing the ocean and a supply of the original cannon balls used by the British for protection against pirates.

We met the curator who gave us a formal tour. There was a charge of 5000 Cedis for still photos and 10,000 for video. Much of the early trade took place from this coast; gold, ivory, pepper, and eventually slaves. Listening to the curator, as he outlined history for us, was heart breaking. As I stood on the grounds of the forte, I could almost feel the torment that my ancestors experienced during their capture. Looking out into the Atlantic Ocean, I stared as though I could see the slave ship as it slowly disappeared on the horizon. According to the curator, the White men had determined that Africans would make good slaves because, as they said, "they had no souls and they were likened to animals."

22

Initially, the Portuguese bought Cape Coast for 64 pounds in 1464. In the 15ᵗʰ century, the Portuguese traded slaves to European nations. Later, with the establishment of the New World, the slave trade intensified. In 1657, the Dutch drove the Portuguese out of Cape Coast. In 1664, the English gained control of Cape Coast. The castle was built of wood, marble, and other imported products from England, and it took 50 years to build. Because the country was so rich in gold, it was called the Gold Coast.

Tourists entering the slave dungeons.

The slaves, many of whom were criminals or prisoners of tribal wars and strong men, walked barefoot 20 miles from Satago to Assin Manso for their last bath. Coming from different areas, the language was not familiar so there was little communication. Some died from exhaustion or attacks by wild animals. They washed in the Donko Nsuo River, otherwise known as the "Slave River." Then, they were prepared for auction by shaving their heads; this would eliminate gray hair and thereby not disclose the age of the slave. The skin was polished with palm oil.

The color of the eyes was checked to determine if there was an illness. The men were struck with canes to make them jump to see how agile they were. The adults were sold for 3 pounds and the youth were sold 3 or 4 together for 3 pounds.

23

About 1000 slaves were held in dungeons for 2 weeks at a time, the males in one dungeon and the females in another. There were receptacles on the wall so the slaves could physically relieve themselves, but because the holding quarters were so cramped and the slaves being chained to the walls, it was difficult to move around. Thus, it became necessary to relieve themselves in their existing positions. Gutters were carved in the floor to drain the feces and urine into the ocean. There is a mark on the wall about 2 feet high to indicate the height of the body excretions at any given time. Many died while detained from malaria, yellow fever, or other disease and were thrown into the ocean.

There was no escape. There were small openings high above the floor for ventilation. Some slaves died before auction due to the conditions. Ironically, there was a chapel over the dungeon where church services were held. The slaves left the dungeon, traveled through a tunnel, and then through a small passageway to board the ship for the New World. That small passageway was called "the door of no return." The slaves faced eternal doom. This was the beginning of history that took our ancestors to the New World as slaves. After slavery was abolished, two runaway slaves had requested to be sent back home, upon their deaths. Sonny Carson (from the US) and Crystal (from Jamaica) were returned home and entombed in Assin Manso. With this move, the passageway that the slaves once exited is now called "the door of return." I, now, feel in honor of my ancestors, I have gone full circle and also returned home.

It is estimated that between 60 million and 300 million slaves were auctioned. Only about 20% survived the trip over to the New World. After the Emancipation in 1873, many Blacks moved back and settled in Liberia. Poverty is considered to be the country's #1 cost of slavery. This was an amazing tour. Today, this castle, of course, is considered one of the most memorable stops on the tour. Looking out onto the Atlantic Ocean, you can see canoes of fishermen as they come and go. Philip Ouapo is entombed inside the male dungeon. He was an Anglican pastor, one of the first to be trained in England. He set up the first school for the children of African women and European men. There is an attendant who sits at his burial site and prays for him daily.

When you walk through the "door of return," there are flags waving across the sky and down below are dozens of women and children aiding the fishermen as they bring in today's catch. I saw a child about 5 years old holding a fish as though he was about the clean it. The women refused pictures of them or the children. We tipped the curator and left. We had one more stop before lunch.

The Elmina Castle

We toured the Elmina Castle, built in 1482, also called "Sa'n Jorge de Mina" meaning St. George of the Mine or "Elmina" the mine. This castle was back in Elmina, and about 10 minutes pass our hotel. Again, this was another extraordinary town.

The buildings here were also designed with an early colonial flavor. The Portuguese were given permission by a chief of a nearby village to build the castle as a trading outpost to provide vessels a secure harbor. This was considered the first castle of it type to be used for slave trade. Reports of over 30, 000 slaves were traded here for products such as silk, beads, knives, guns and linens. In 1642, the Dutch captured the castle and later the English took over.

As we got off the tour bus, the vendors bombarded us with items for sale. On the way into the castle, I met 2 young brothers, Paul and Randy, around 12 and 15 years of age. The tour guides told us that many of the students quit school to sell items but it is discouraged so they did not want us to buy from the kids. But Paul and Randy did not have anything for sale.

While I was inside the castle, they apparently got a seashell from the ocean inscribed, "To Mother Dorothy, enjoy your stay and have a safe trip back home. God Bless, you." Paul handed me the seashell through the window of the bus and I gave him a t-shirt with the word "Cozumel" across the front. We did exchange e-mail addresses. Yahoo is the popular Internet search engine there.

I started the tour but left to mingle with the street vendors. There were interesting conversations with the lady vendors. For instance, one Sister sold beads that are typically, tied around the waist of the young female. As the child grows, the beads help to monitor her waist and shape her figure. The beads, apparently, work because the women have beautiful shapes. The teenage girls are also very shapely. As the ladies become adults, they continue to wear the beads as body jewelry. Some of the ladies jumped on this purchase, but I, not seeing the value, did not.

Point of Interest...
The Beads
When I returned to Greensboro, I stopped by Baluba's African Market. That store has the most magnificent pieces of art. They also had the beads like the ones the lady vendor was selling in Ghana. I purchased a couple of them just to experiment. I do not wear much jewelry because it feels annoying to my skin. These beads are worn 24-7, when you sleep, and when you shower. I am pleased to report that I have been wearing the beads more than a month. They do not aggravate me. Because I am aware that they are there, I am conscious of my posture. I usually measure my waistline a couple of times a month. The beads help to monitor my waistline. I can see how they help to shape the woman's figure.

The Shopping Mall
Journal Entry...
We had lunch and went back to the shopping mall. Today was an interesting day. All week, we had seen school kids in uniforms, peach colored shirts and brown pants, skirts, or jumpers. Some students were here at the shopping mall, enjoying the PANAFEST activities. In addition to the clothing and art vendors are food vendors.

26

There was also a booth, I think a radio station, promoting activities for the week and making strong announcements in support of HIV/AIDS Awareness. The person speaking was encouraging people to come by their booth to pick up fliers. Some of the school kids stopped by for fliers and then took their seats in the bleachers under the direction of their teachers.

Education

The tour guides told us that students have to pay for school. It cost $80 a year for elementary and middle school students and $100 a year for high school students. Private school cost more. Of course, many cannot afford to pay for school and thus, drop out. The school system is divided into four levels. Pre-school education lasts for two years, mostly urban children.

Primary education, from the age 6 to the age 12, lasts for 6 years, followed by Junior Secondary School (JSS) which lasts for three years of academic training, combined with technical and vocational training. Those continuing on go to Senior Secondary School (SSS) for 3 years. Following completion of SSS, students must pass the Basis Education Certification Exam for entrance into the universities. Overall enrollment is down over the last decade; most children only complete Basic Education.

Parents and students are losing motivation to attend school because it is difficult to get a decent job, particularly with the government without completing SSS. But if they can not afford to attend SSS, why spend money to attend JSS. Primary and JSS are considered together as Basic Education, and the government is considering a program of compulsory basic education for all children when enough teachers and facilities are available. Students are taught local vernacular until they reach JSS, then they are taught English.

The students were very neat. According to beliefs, it is rude for the females to relax or style their hair with braids or otherwise, until age 18. Because it is difficult to manage their hair, many of the females will cut their hair as low as the males until they reach the acceptable age to style it differently. I had an opportunity to take a picture with the school kids. This was a monumental opportunity for the students and for me. It was a thrill!

Many of them got paper and pens so that we could exchange addresses. My impression of the kids was that they were very polite. Some of them were a little camera shy, initially, but they seemed to enjoy the contact with the outside world. We left for the hotel at 1600 hours. We needed to rest and have an early dinner in order to leave for the evening activities back at Cape Coast Castle. Dinner, again, was familiar.

Point of Interest...

The following is a chart outlining enrollment in 1992/93 vs. 2001/2003:

Enrollment

Level of Schools	1992/93	2002/03
Preschool	no statistics	no statistics
Primary School	1.8 million	1.3 million
Junior Secondary School	629,258	489,000
Senior Secondary School	247,496	107,600

In 1957, when the nation gained its independence, there were a handful of primary and secondary schools and one university. The most recent figures show the following #s:

Level of Schools	# of Schools	Teacher/Student Ratio 1992/93
Preschool	no statistics	no statistics
Primary Schools	12,130	30
Junior Secondary Schools	5,450	19
Senior Secondary Schools	503	22
Training Colleges		21
Technical Institutions		18
Universities	16	5

SSS consist of day students as well as boarders. The 2001-2002 school year reported day student tuition was 49,000 Cedis, and the boarders paid 443,000 Cedis.

Many of the schoolbooks have been donated. One report shows that SSS lack enough Science books. Some schools have an excess amount of books that are not used because they are not right for the course. Efforts to increase the level of skills and education are underway. It has been reported that 60% of the rural population in Ghana have no electricity in their homes. This is an opportunity to increase technology through the use of solar energy.

Scholarships are granted to Teacher Trainees in Accra Training and Presbyterian Women's Training in Accra. It is expected that the trainees will complete school and fill some of the vacancies where the services are needed. Best Teacher awards are given to the top 10 deserving teachers in Primary, JSS, and SSS. Awards consist of gas stoves, sound systems, and suitcases. These incentives are used to retain good teachers and motivate them to do their best.

A Science, Technology, and Mathematics Education Clinic recently opened at Abura-Asebu-Kwaman, Kese' District in the Central Region at Cape Coast. The clinic was opened for the students, however, the teachers need improved Science skills in order to teach the students.

Back to Cape Coast Castle
Journal Entry...
It was dark as we arrived at the castle around 1930 hours. Everyone converged at Mfantsipim Junction to line up for the 2 mile candlelight vigil through the streets of Cape Coast leading up to the castle. This was the beginning of the evening activities at the castle.

Once we walked through the streets up to the castle, a host of dignitaries led us into the courtyard. There was President Kufuor, the King of Ghana and his entourage, Minister of Tourism (Jake Obetsebi-Lamptey) and his associates, and African American Delegates led by Dr. Leonard Jeffries.

According to a GNA news article dated 29-07-03, Jake Obetsebi-Lamptey said "Africans living in the Diaspora, probably have more to give in the way of skills, which the African Continent urgently needs. He pointed out that the home continent remains the fount to constantly recharge the values that distinguish us as Africans." Dr. Jeffries is an African-American lecturer at the Department of African Studies at the City College of New York. In the same article, Dr Jeffries stated that "Ghana has a special responsibility to unite all Africans, especially those in the Diaspora. It is her sacred mission to re-establish all Africans to their ancestral roots."

Our guides had arranged seating for us, although a few of us stole seats up front near the dignitaries. Here, at night under the stars was more spiritual than during the day. The program began around 2200 hours. There was a moving theatrical production called "Human Cargo." This was an "epigraph" to the occurrence of slave trade and human transportation from Black Africa across the Atlantic to the United States of America. It was a portrayal of a harrowing experience and the natural human desire to attain freedom from an inhuman institution. It also depicted the tenacity of ideas of subjugation by one human being over another. It was written and directed by Fred Agbeyegbe of Ajo Productions of Nigeria.

Spiritual Songstress Kay Boyd from Mount Vernon, New York offered a very moving musical selection. There was a dance by The Cuban National Dancers. At 0000 hours, the royal procession, with lighted candles, entered the male dungeon to lay a wreath in honor of our ancestors. Afterwards, there was Proclamation of Emancipation Day and prayer. The program was over and we left. Each day after our tour, we would have a question and answer session with the tour guides. There were plenty of questions thrown at them tonight. We were all wondering how to get this message back home to others. Everyone needs to experience what we have just experienced. The Ghanaians are trying to reunite the Blacks around the world.

If the 20% of slaves who survived the trip over to the New World represent most of the ancestry of Blacks outside of Africa, our roots are there and we have to go back and visit the Motherland. Twice, I heard today from our African Brothers and Sisters that we are not considered African Americans, but Africans who live in America. There has never been a more true statement.

Over the years, we have been wrestling with our identity. We have gone from Coloreds to Negroes, to Afro Americans, and now African Americans. We are just Africans who live in America. At this point, I decided that I would do my part to share my experiences. What a day!

Day VII
Friday 01-08-03

Surely oppression maketh a wise man mad;
and a gift destroyeth the heart.
Better is the end of a thing than the beginning
thereof;
And the patient in spirit is better than the
proud in spirit.
Be not hasty in thy spirit to be angry; for anger
resteth in the bosom of fools.
Ecclesiastes 7:7-9

Emancipation Day

Journal Entry...

For the British West Indies, which started the celebration of Emancipation Day, the abolition came in the Emancipation Act passed by the British Parliament in 1833 to become effective on 1st August 1834. Emancipation for the Africans from the British Caribbean, Brazil, America, and others, meant freedom, the liberty to move freely from place to place, live on their own, work for themselves and not at the command of someone else. At this point, as I mentioned earlier, many moved back to Africa. Ghana has celebrated Emancipation Day on 1st August annually since 1998, and it has a growing popularity each year.

On this day, We traveled to Assin Manso to see the "Slave River" and the grave sites of the two former slaves from the US and Jamaica who were returned home. Afterwards, across the street was the Emancipation Day Ceremony. Several of the women had worn their new African attire in anticipation of this event. This was a grand, colorful, and spectacular event that showcased the pomp and pageantry of Ghana's traditional rulers. The event was held on a recreation field and chairs were set up in a square under tents. The visitors were accommodated and the school kids stood behind our seats. I recognized my young friend by the t-shirt I had given him the day before as well as many others from previous events.

The Ashante King, Otumfuo Osei Tutu II, entered with his entourage. He was laced with heavy layers of gold around his neck and on his hand and he was draped in beautiful black and white Kente cloth. His entourage included his servants. Someone carried his golden stool. According to myth, during the 17th century, a high priest, named Anokye, caused a golden stool to descend from the sky to seal the union of the Ashante people. Thus, each new King inherits the stool. Another person carried his huge red parasol. Other members included the chiefs and their servants carrying parasols, with drummers and horn blowers bringing up the rear of the procession. The entire procession must have consisted of 100 people.

Sonny Carson and Crystal

The US Delegation was there and all of the Black Sisters and Brothers visiting from around the world were invited to come to the center ground. There

33

must have been about 200 of us. We were applauded and thanked for taking part in the event. There was a small percentage of Whites there. Some were married to Blacks and some were missionaries. There were perhaps a few others who were just interested in seeing what was taking place. There was also a slave bath ceremony that took place at the "Slave River" and wreaths were also placed at the graves of Sonny Carson and Crystal.

Point of Interest…
The Ashante King, Otumfuo Osei Tutu II

Although there are dozens of tribes in Ghana, the Ashante Empire headed by Otumfuo Osei Tutu II, is by far the most popular. Otumfuo Osei Tuto II, the 16th Ashante King, was born 5 May 1950 in Kumasi. He was one of 5 children. He attended secondary school in a town in the Western Region of Ghana.

This gave him an opportunity to learn more about Ghana and the outside world of poverty. He continued his studies at Kilburn Polytechnic in Northwest London and the University of North London. He is married and has 3 children. The King's immediate predecessor had already broken the 300-year tradition of multiple wives. Before becoming king, Otumfuo Osei Tutu II worked in Britain and Canada then he became an entrepreneur and set up a business importing mining equipment from Britain and South Africa for the Ashanti Goldfields Company.

He is more approachable than his predecessors. He is considered to be modern but still observes Ashante traditions. For instance, he can not eat or drink in public, not even speak. That is why he has a linguist. He has a high regard for education. He recently contributed a 10 million Cedi scheme for the University of Ghana's Institute of Professional Studies, 10 million Cedi scheme for Osei Kyeretwie Secondary School in Kumasi, a 2 million Cedi scheme for the Presbyterian Church in Kumasi for its education week; and 5 million Cedis for the Sefwi Wiawso Secondary School where he attended as a boy.

The king is an avid golfer, he loves reading, and he is a stanch supporter of the Ashante Kotoka Football Club. The Ashanti population is huge and difficult to rule due to the wide range of political views. The new King has instituted committees among the governing councils to help drive public focus in a simultaneous direction.

His father, Nana Boakye Danquah (now 85 years old) belongs to a group within the Palace military organization called Atuntufuo- a bodyguard company for the King. Tradition dictates that the father remove his sandals and fold his cloth to waist level as a sign of homage when talking to the King. Nana Afua Kobi

34

Serwaa Ampem II, the king's mother, has been the queen mom for 22 years. She has the responsibility of choosing the new king. The king's children are not royal bloods. The next king would be a child of the king's aunt or another relative. The king holds court on Mondays and Thursday for situations involving the men and the queen mom holds court on Tuesdays for situations involving the women.

Journal Entry...

After the event, we left for one more stop at the shopping mall, but first the ladies needed to make another transfer of money. Can you believe there were still items to be purchased? A couple of the ladies had bought so much that the vendors gave them complimentary items. I told one lady that on her return trip there would be a billboard welcoming her back to town.

That night, since we had eaten the same food all week, the group leader suggested that we go to Mabel's Table Restaurant, a short distance from the hotel. The ladies were in agreement and understood that this meal would not be covered under the 2 meal per day agreement. When we got back to the hotel, we stopped by the buffet for dessert. Sure enough, dinner was familiar. They had served the same meal all week, alternating occasionally with beef or chicken.

Afterwards, I went to the room to shampoo my hair. Before leaving the states, I purchased a 220 adapter to use with my electrical appliances. Several of the ladies in the group had purchased the wrong adapter. I had gone by the Radio Shack and purchased the 1600-Watt Foreign Travel Voltage Converter. It worked for my steam iron and my soft curlers. The others borrowed it for their video cameras.

This was a nice resort but the service was poor. The maid service did not leave wash cloths (or maybe that is the norm). I had to request twice before I got one. The next day, I had to beg all over again. So, when I did get the next one, I held on to it until I left. In the future, it would behoove me to bring my own wash cloths.

Day VIII
Saturday 02-08-03

Then I beheld the work of God, that a man
cannot find out the work that is done under the
sun; because though a man labour to seek it
out; yet
he shall not find it, yea further; though a wise
man think to know it,
yet shall he not be able to find it.
Ecclesiastes 8:17

Kumasi

Journal Entry...
    We checked out of the Elmina Beach Resort enroute to Kumasi that is about a 3 hour ride inland. Rest rooms were not very accessible so if we needed to stop, we had to mention it early so the driver could stop accordingly. The tour guide led a discussion as we traveled.

    Kumasi has a population of 1.8 million people. It is the Capital of the Ashanti Region, home of the Ashanti people (more commonly spelled Ashante). Ashanti is a spelling used during the pre-independence era. The people in this area are the richest and most powerful tribe in Ghana.

36

It was settled in the 16th century and today is the 2nd largest city in Ghana. Kumasi was the central point of Slave Trade as its King traded his prisoners for weapons, ammunition and other wares. Kumasi is also known as the Garden City because of its tree lined streets and the beautiful flower gardens. The people are surrounded by legends and colorful history. The tour guide shared some beliefs of all the people in general. The following is a list that can be shared by us all:

Popular Beliefs that we can all live by

1. When a man is drunk, he cannot see the hawk.
If you don't understand the process, you cannot make change.

2. No matter how long a piece of wood lies in the pond, it will never be a crocodile.
If it is not in the soul, it is not real.

3. Stolen joy is temporary, look for joy everlasting.
Joy at someone else's expense is temporary.

4. He who has no teeth should not fight over bones.
Do not fight a battle that you know you cannot win.

Point of Interest…
Kofi Annan

Kofi Annan, the 7th Secretary General of the United Nations, was born in kumasi 8 April 1938. He studied Economics at the University of Science and Technology in Kumasi and earned a Master's Degree at Macalester College in St. Paul, Minnesota in the US.

He did graduate work in Geneva and earned a Master's degree in Management from MIT in 1972. He was the first to be elected from the ranks of UN Staff. He was elected for a second term on 1 January 2000, ending 31 December 2006.

He joined the UN in 1962 as Administrative and Budget Officer with the World Health Organization (WHO) in Geneva. He has also served in many other capacities leading up to the appointment. He is fluent in English, French and several African Languages. He is married to Nane Annan, of Sweden, a lawyer and artist. She has 2 issues of concern, HIV/AIDS and the education of women. Mr. and Mrs. Annan have 3 children.

Obuasi

Journal Entry...

We drove through Obuasi (Obwa'se), located about 200km NW of Accra. Obuasi is deemed the richest town in the world because of the gold mountains. Driving through, to the right, we could see mountains with vegetation but we were informed that those were mountains of gold.

There was an overhead receptacle that channeled the gold from the mountain to an extraction refinery. It has a population of more than 70,000 people (1984 reports). Local people have extracted gold here since the 1700's. By the 1890's, the Europeans had developed the town into a mining town and the Ashanti Goldfields Corporation (AGC) was established in London in 1897.

AGC is an African based international gold mining and exploration group with six producing mines in four African countries, Ghana, Guinea, Tanzania, and Zimbabwe. The mines in which the group has interest have 44 million ounces of measured and indicated gold resources. The company was the first African company to be placed on the NYSE. It is also listed on the Zimbabwe Stock exchange, as well as the London and the US exchange. The government owns about 17% of the gold shares, the British own 33 %, and the remaining shares are owned by other investors.

We could tell the difference in the economic structure as we drove through the villages, there were antennas on the roofs of about every house, too obvious to miss. This meant that there were television sets, and even more—electricity. There were also red brick apartment buildings that were rare, but we were told that the British had these built for the miners. The life style was definitely upgraded in this area.

Around 1400 hours, we approached Kumasi. The first stop was the king's palace. We were not able to tour the current living quarters of the King, but the older facility was available for tour. I walked through a portion of it.

There were waxed sculptures of the previous King and the Queen Mom, the mother of the King, and some weapons used during previous battles. It was not as impressive, I am sure, as the current king's living quarters.

We missed lunch while we were traveling, so around 1600 hours we decided to check into the hotel and have lunch there. We arrived at The Georgia Hotel. On the exterior, it appeared to be a decent enough hotel, although not as nice as the previous ones. Upon entry, I knew I would not be as pleased here.

On the wall at the front desk was a plaque "1993 hotel of the year." Obviously, the next 10 years of existence was based on the merit of this plaque. Renovation had begun. The bathrooms had been tiled and they each had a bidet. My view out of the window was 2nd floor construction. There was a little water on the bathroom floor and the odor of mildew. I wanted to request another room but my roommate reminded me that I was not in the states. I accepted her observation. There was a small business center. I paid 500 Cedis per minute to e-mail my family back home.

The tour guides suggested that we attend an Ashanti funeral because they were so different from in the states. My roommate stated that she had just buried her husband 4 months earlier and had no intentions of going to another funeral just yet, so I stayed behind with her. The others left around 1630 hours to attend the funeral. My roommate and I had dinner around 1730 hours on the patio at the pool.

This was a nice little setting. The servants were young men and women around 18 years of age. Whenever we had dinner, I was sure to talk with the waiters and waitresses. I would get their names and carry on little small talk that would make them smile. They all had such nice, pretty teeth. The menu consisted of fish, cabbage, spicy red rice, and a cup of vanilla ice cream. I learned later that the spicy red rice is called Jollof Rice. It must be a popular dish because it was served at each of the other hotels. Everyone serves the white rice in a mound. It appeared that a bowl was filled with rice and then turned over on the plate to form a mound. Even though I had eaten some of the same foods at the other hotels, the food was prepared in a way to give it some originality.

When the others returned, they excitedly discussed the funeral. A hotel owner had died about 6 months earlier. He was preserved until the funeral. There were about a thousand people in attendance. Many of them were chiefs and their entourage that were seen at the festivities the day before. There were dancers and drummers. Traditional colors for funerals are black and white for the men and women. The traditional Adinkra cloth for funerals is Eyie (meaning farewell). All of the ladies agreed that it was definitely worth attending. A homecoming celebration is held at church for the deceased on the day following the funeral.

After dinner, the group leader suggested that we attend church on Sunday and again wear our African attire. All of the ladies agreed and some departed to prepare for church. One of the ladies' had brought a deck of playing cards, so the rest of us decided to play a game of Bid Whiz. For about 1 ½ hours, we played, all admitting that it had been awhile since our last game.

We stumbled through a few hands, some forgetting the rules, others making up the rules as they played. Finally, we decided that the game was over. We each called it a night and went up stairs. This was not a good night for me because of the odor of mildew in the room. I had to sleep with the fan on all night and I kept my head under the covers because it was very, very cold.

Day IX
Sunday 03-08-03

I returned, and saw under the sun, that the race
is not to the swift,
Nor the battle to the strong, neither yet
bread to the wise,
Nor yet riches to men of understanding; nor
yet favour to men of skill;
But time and chance happeneth to them all.
Ecclesiastes 9:11

International Central Gospel Church

Journal Entry...

We left for church around 0800 hours. We were not coming back to the hotel after church, so we had to take changing clothes and shoes. As it turned out, this was a church that one of the tour guides attended. This was an outdoor facility. There was a roof with blue canvass attached to the roof. I imagine it is pulled down when it rains. The sermon had not started. Aside from the facility, it felt like church back home. There were drums, guitars, keyboard, and a great sound system.

41

Many of the female members were wearing African attire. Most of the men wore suits and ties. The minister and the first lady were in African attire. The ladies in the choir wore blue 2-piece suits and the men wore suits and ties. It was obvious, the choir was preparing for the Spirit of The Lord. They were singing, shouting, and having a joyous time. We took seats where available and joined in. Tears came to my eyes when I heard the choir sing, "Awesome God," by Michael W. Smith. I knew that I was home. Our Father is everywhere and He made a way for me to see Him there in all of His glory. These people on this depressed and forgotten continent still find reason and cause to worship God.

Lyrics from "Awesome God"

Our God is an awesome God
He reigns from Heaven above,
With wisdom, power, and love,
Our God is an awesome God.

A short while later, the ushers moved us to the front row and we were formally introduced. On the way to church, the group had discussed singing a rendition of "Kumbah Ya, My Lord." The tour guide had talked with the minister and told him that we wanted to sing a song. One of our group members was Minister of Music at her church. She led the song and we joined in on the chorus. We were awesome! We got a standing ovation. Then, the minister delivered a powerful sermon. There were about 5 offerings and monetary gift requests. At this point, it really felt like home. It was 1ˢᵗ Sunday so we shared in Communion. A couple brought their baby to the front to be christened. Church was over around 1030 hours. Many of the members came to greet us and shook our hands.

We went to Jofel Restaurant and Catering Service for lunch. Many of the ladies ordered chicken and chips. This seemed to work for them. I think all enjoyed.

Bonwire (Kente Village)
After lunch, we went to Bonwire, also known as the Kente Village. This is the home of the Kente cloth. As the story goes, two farmers watched a spider spin a web for two weeks and came up with the idea to weave the Kente cloth. We watched the men as they wove. The cloth is woven on a narrow horizontal loom. It is woven on a narrow strip about 3-5 inches wide and 5-6 feet long. Several strips are sewn together to make a wider piece of cloth for both men and women. A man's cloth may contain up to 24 strips and measures about 5x6 feet. The woman's two-piece cloth may contain 8-12 strips each piece.

42

The warp threads are laid in such a fashion to give a name and meaning to the cloth. These names and meanings affect Akan beliefs, historical events, social and political organizations in the Akan Society, or may be named after people.

The cloth can be purchased with a single weave, double weave, and a triple weave. The Asante weaver refers to Kente as nwentoma (woven cloth) to distinguish it from the factory made cloth (ntoma) and the Adinkra cloth that is stamped (ntiama ntoma) by the block print technique.

The largest known Kente cloth, measuring about 12x20 feet, is the piece Ghana presented to the United Nations in 1960. The cloth is called Tikoro nko agyima, which means one head does not constitute a council. The cloth can be purchased here at the village. The vendors are eager to sell the cloth. The prices range from 90,000 Cedis for the single weave and upwards to 180,000 Cedis or more for the double and triple weave. Keep in mind that you can barter a little for the material.

From here, we needed a restroom break. There was not a facility in this area so the tour driver suggested that we go to the Chief's village nearby. This was a nice facility. There was a white gate that surrounded the village. There was a main residential facility and a gift shop. We used the restroom off from the gift shop. This was the Chief in charge of the King's wardrobe. He had nice pieces of cloth for sale in the gift shop. One lady, in the group, bought material for a bedspread. Another lady bought material for a tablecloth. Normally, we would have tipped the chief for the use of his facility, but because we made purchases, he waived the tip.

Ntonso (Home of Adinkra Cloth)

We also visited Ntonso, home of the handprinted Adinkra cloth. We observed the stages involved in printing the Adinkra symbols on to plain fabrics using wooden stamps. This material is not supposed to be washed. Adinkra is one of the highly valued hand-printed and hand-embroidered cloths. Its origin is traced to the Ashante people of Ghana and the Gyaman people of Cote d'Ivoire (Ivory Coast). By the 19th century, the Ashante people had begun to develop their own unique art in Adinkra printing. Originally, Adinkra cloths were made and used exclusively by the royal and spiritual leaders for sacred ceremonies and rituals. Today, the material is used and worn by all for festivals, weddings, churchgoing, and other ceremonies. Each of the designs that make up the Adinkra symbols represents a proverb, historical event, or human attitude.

43

Ahwiaa (The Wood Carvers Village)

Next, we toured and shopped at Ahwiaa, the wood carvers' village known for making Ashanti Stools and Akuaba Fertility Dolls. The fertility dolls are supposed to help women with fertility problems. No one bought a doll. One of the ladies bought the Ashanti stool. A replica of the original Ashanti stool is handcarved and made of Sese wood. It may carry the design of any of the Adinkra symbols, such as, the Sankofa (means never forget where you came from), the Gye Nyeme (Accept God), and Crocodile (crossed crocodiles, we share one stomach but we fight over food).

I believe it was too late in the day to shop and the vendors were a little too aggressive. So, we headed back to the hotel. When I got to my room, there was a puddle in the bathroom from the previous leak. I told my roommate that I would not be staying that night. She agreed and we got another room. Dinner was the same as the night before but instead of ice cream, we had watermelon. Before we left the dining area, the tour guide mentioned that a former chief was on the premises if we wanted to meet him. He was an older reserved, gentleman. He shook hands with the first lady and said, "I am going to marry you." Two or three of the ladies sat down to talk with him and the rest of us went to our rooms.

Day X
Monday 04-08-03

Curse not the King, no not in thy thought;
And curse not the rich in thy bedchamber;
For a bird of the air shall carry the voice,
And that which hath wings shall tell the matter.
Ecclesiastes 10:20

The Naming Ceremony

Journal Entry...

This ceremony was performed at 0800 hours. This is an Ashanti ceremony to obtain an African name for the day. The ladies wore their African attire for this ceremony. It was held at the chief's village. I was not as impressed with this village as the one before. The chief had a linguist who translates for him. However, the linguist could not speak English so there was a stand-in linguist. The chief apologized for having us there so early but he had to leave for the King's court by 0900 hours. The chief also had a servant who accompanied him.

We provided the chief with a beverage for the ceremony. The guide and the group leader had previously arranged this. He made a few statements that the linguist translated. Then he drank from a cup. He then passed a drink around for each of us to take a sip. We had provided our dates of birth in advance to determine the day of the week in which we were born.

From this, the chief could determine our soul name or Kradin based on the understanding that the day on which a child is born is the day that the baby's soul decided to come forth into the world.

Day	Mon	Tues	Wed	Thurs	Fri	Sat	Sun
Male	Kwadwo	Kwabena	Kwaku	Yaw	Kofi	Kwame	Kwasi
Female	Adwowa	Abena	Akua	Yaa	Afua	Ama	Akosua

The day you were born can also designate your personality:

Sunday	Protector
Monday	very careful, weigh the pros and cons
Tuesday	Curious
Wednesday	Intelligent, creative
Thursday	Brave
Friday	Intellectual
Saturday	Born Leader

Your name can also be determined if you were born on a sacred day, based on human behavior, or your occupational background. Each of us stood before the chief, he gave us an African name for the day and explained its purpose as we held a ceremonious dagger. I was born on Wednesday, I am the, intelligent, creative one and was named Nana Nyarko, a Queen Mom. We received a naming certificate from the Royal Palace of Asem - Kumasi, Ghana. We tipped the Chief and left.

We needed to get back to the hotel to pack up and head back to Accra. It was about a 4-hour trip back. There was some discussion about the naming ceremony as we traveled and then most of us slept. When we got back, we stopped by the hotel. The tour guides took our luggage in and got us checked in. Then we headed out to a jewelry store. The ladies had wanted to purchase jewelry in the gold capital (Obuasi) but it was not possible during the weekend.

The first stop was not very impressive. There was not an ample supply of jewelry. Then we went to Said's Jewelers. This jewelry was nice and the ladies decided that they could buy here. They bought rings and bracelets, and necklaces. The jewelry was measured and sold for $20 per gram for 18 carat. This was not a bad price.

The ladies seemed to be pleased with their purchases. The tour guides were very protective of us. They said that it was an opportunity for us to be mugged just coming out of a jewelry shop.

We were there about 2 hours and then headed back to the hotel. There was a sign on the marquee outside of the hotel advertising Soul Food Aug 4-6. We were all looking forward to some good old soul food after several days of the same food. We were informed when we got back to the hotel that we would be eating outside the hotel. This was disappointing to all of us. I was tired and did not want to get back on the bus. The group leader had the tour guide to call the agency and explain the dilemma. As it turned out, the agency had already paid a percentage of the food bill and the guide had a check for the remaining amount owed. So we had to go.

This night, we went to the Indigo Restaurant, which was right across from the American Embassy. There was an outside patio restaurant upstairs and a club downstairs. It was a nice restaurant except there was not a lot of light. I had a waiter to bring 2 candles for the table, but because of the night breeze, they did not last very long.

The menu consisted of Red Snapper, Jollof rice and white rice, cabbage, beef, and chicken. Dessert consisted of watermelon and pineapple. It was a nice presentation. This was the first time that I had Red Snapper. He laid there staring at me as I cut into his stomach for my portion. My roommate said, "I don't know about anyone else but I thought the food was great." She had become the official food critic of the group.

When we got back to the hotel, we went down stairs to the bar to meet an old classmate of one of our group members whom now lives in Ghana. She was donning a beautiful African outfit. She is a Bennett Belle, graduated from Bennett College in Greensboro, NC. She married a Ghanaian, moved there in the mid-sixties and raised her children there. She said that once her children graduated from high school, they returned to the states to attend college. Only one child returned to Ghana after completing college. She is a member of the African American Associations of Ghanaians (AAAG). She said that there are a lot more African Americans who have moved to the area.

I also met another African American from D.C. who now lives in Ghana and also a member of AAAG. She was responsible for preparing the Soul Food for the hotel. She said she prepares the food a couple of times a year. The menu consisted of anything and everything you can think of.

47

She said that one man from the states likes his cornbread without sugar so she had to prepare a special pan without sugar. She wants to keep everyone happy. The AAAG has prepared a cookbook for sale to coincide with the cultural special. I mentioned to her that we had attended the naming ceremony earlier that day and that I did not take it too seriously. But she informed me that it is a very serious ceremony. This is the procedure used when people move there and want to change their names back to a traditional African name. Boy, was there pie in my face!

My roommate and I went to the casino for a while. She was pretty good on the slot machines. The last few times that I have played the slots, my luck had been lousy. Therefore, I spent very little money trying to win. Afterwards, we retired for the evening. It had been a long day.

Point of Interest...
Maya Angelou

Ms. Angelou was born in 1928 as Marguerite Johnson in St. Louis and was raised in Arkansas. She began her career as a dancer and actor. She has added to her credits; author, songwriter, director and producer. She was married to a South African and lived in Cairo where she was editor of the Arab Observer, the only English language news in the Middle East.

In Ghana, she was a feature editor for the African Review and taught at the University of Ghana until 1966 when she returned to the states at the request of Dr. Martin Luther King to become a Coordinator for the Southern Christian Leadership Conference. She has published 10 best selling books including her autobiography "I Know Why the Caged Bird Sings."

Day XI
Tuesday 05-08-03

Truly the light is sweet, and a pleasant thing it is
for the eyes to behold the sun;
But if a man live many years, and
rejoice in them all; yet let him remember the
days of darkness; for they shall be many.
All that cometh is vanity.
Ecclesiastes 11:7-8

Aburi Botanical Gardens

Journal Entry...

We left around 1000 hours and traveled through Accra up to Aburi Mountains. I had asked the guide earlier about the President of Accra. He wanted to wait until we were back in Accra to cover current issues. The current President of Ghana is John Agyekum Kufuor. As with all governments, there are the pros and cons. The lead tour guide began the conversation regarding the politics. The driver, who had not said much during the entire trip, cut in and started to speak in their native language. We could not understand verbatim but by the sound and expressions, we could tell there was dissention.

Apparently, the leader was opposed to some things that happened with a previous president but the driver and the other guide felt differently. Beyond that, the conversation began to cease, particularly as we headed up the winding roads of the mountains. As the driver became more intense, he seemed to drive a little faster. We had to remind him to slow down. Then we all had a big laugh. From this point on, the lead guide took a minor role. He seemed to have become upset with the other two guides.

Looking down into the valley, as we traveled, was breath taking. It was so beautiful to look down at the beautiful green foliage below. We stopped to take pictures and saw women on the slope of a hill breaking up rocks. One had a baby with her. A hotel was being built there and these ladies were apparently hired to break up the rocks for the foundation. When they saw us, they ran up the slope to greet us. Some members of the group took pictures of them. Afterwards, the ladies wanted compensation for the pictures. Some group members gave money. One lady gave them a bag of tuna and other items. They were overjoyed and then left, headed back down the slope.

We passed a compound that was built by a former president for meetings with diplomats. This would be the equivalent to Camp David in the US. We could see it from the road but there was a guard at the entrance so that was as close as we got. We passed a facility owned by Marie Marley, Bob Marley's wife. It is intended to be a recording studio but it had not opened yet. As with any life in the mountains, the homes were very nice and the view was magnificent.

We arrived at the Aburi Botanical Gardens. Aburi is about 30 miles north of Accra. Still pictures were 5000 Cedis and video cameras were 30,000 Cedis. Our guide was Cecelia. She had worked there for about 15 years. This garden was several acres of land donated by several townspeople. The temperature was quite mild and the garden had a tropical flavor, literally.

There were all kinds of trees. We saw Cinnamon, Cocoa, Camphor, Rubber, Banana, Cola, Pineapple, Coconut, and Mango trees. There was also an Incense tree, and an All Spice tree. I thought All Spice was a combination of spices but there is actually a tree called All Spice. Some of the tree leaves could be used for medicinal purposes.

As we walked, there on the ground was a type of vegetation that would fold up and open again when you touched it. There were chalets and a restaurant on the premises and an old airplane on the grounds that the children can play in.

For the first time since we arrived, there was a consistent rain so we visited the gift shop and left. As we traveled back down the parkway, we stopped at the Aburi Craft Market.

The art was more fascinating than any that we had seen before. The statues were larger, some of them 5ft tall. There was a carving of a man who looked like my preacher and I know that carver has never seen him.

One of the ladies became so enthralled with the art that she purchased (2) 5-foot tall carvings, not considering how she would get them back to the states. She got them at such a good deal, she did not think beyond that. They were so large, the only place to store them, as we traveled the rest of the day, was in the isle of the bus. We all agreed that this should have been an earlier stop because the carvings were so unique and the vendors were not nearly as aggressive.

Point of Interest...
The Political System

Ghana won its independence in 1957, and the Preventive Detention Act was passed in 1958. The Act gave power to the Prime Minister to detain people for up to five years and it was used to detain the opponents of the current regime. But, It was seen as a restriction of individual freedom and human rights. On 1 July 1960, Ghana became a republic, one party system (CPP), one president. Dr. Nkrumah was the 1st president. An increase in taxes and a decrease in prices paid to farmers by the government enraged a population of people already opponents of the president. This led to the government being overthrown in 1966 by armed forces.

The National Liberation Council (NLC) was formed to administer the country, lead by Lt. General Joseph Arthur Ankrah. General Ankrah was removed from office in 1969. Lt. General Akwasi Amankwa Afrifa became chairman of the NLC until Edward Akufo Addo became president. The government was overthrown again on 4 June 1979 in a revolt headed by Jerry Rawlings. Dr. Hilla Limann, leader of the Peoples National Party (PNP), became president on 24 September 1979. Dr. Limann was overthrown 31 December 1981 by a coup led by Lt. Jerry Rawlings and the National Democratic Congress (NDC). Rawlings led the country and the NDC, leading to his election as president in 1992.

The current legal system is based on English Common Law and Customary Law. The government is a Constitutional Democracy with a Judicial Branch that is headed by the Supreme Court and a Parliament. The Parliament consists of 200 seats and members are elected for a 4-year term.

In 1992, the people voted for a two party political system. The President would be elected for a period of 4 years and be eligible for re-election of 1 additional term. The Executive Branch consists of the President and his Cabinet Members.

The following is a list of some of the Political Parties:

PNP	Peoples National Party
NCD	National Commission for Democracy
NPP	New Patriotic Party
NDC	National Democratic Congress
EGLE	Every Ghanaian Living Everywhere
CPP	Convention People's Party

President Jerry John Rawlings

Jerry John Rawlings was educated at Achimota School where he obtained his General Certificate of Education in 1966. He enlisted as a flight pilot and became a cadet in the Ghana Air Force in August 1967. He was subsequently selected for officer cadet training at the Ghana Military Academy and Training School, Teshie, in Accra. Flt-Lt. Rawlings ceased to be a member of the Ghana Armed Forces on September 14, 1992.

He formed the National Democratic Congress, and as a result, he won the 1992 Presidential and Parliamentary elections. He and the party again won the 1996 elections. Rawlings did not have some of the intellectual credentials as some political leaders. He did receive an Honorary Doctor of Law Degree from Medgar Evers College at the City University of New York and a Doctorate Degree for Diplomacy and Development at Lincoln University.

He was a people's leader, a common place leader who could relate to the common citizen. He was reported to be the type to smoke half a cigarette and place the other half behind his ear until later, characteristic of a blue-collar worker. One report was that he did not have the greatest understanding of the economics, he just understood when he was hungry.

He is credited with bolstering employment, providing housing, safe water and emphasis on healthcare to rural area. Overall food production has steadily increased over the last decade and Ghana has achieved self-sufficiency in 3 staple crops: maize, cassava, and yams. Therefore, he acquired a legacy well respected among the common people.

President John Kufuor

President Kufuor unsuccessfully ran against President Rawlings in 1996. By the year 2000, Rawlings had exhausted his 2-term restriction. Kufuor did succeed on his second attempt and took office in January 2001. He was the first elected President in Ghanaian history to succeed another elected president. John Agyekum Kufuor was born on December 8, 1938 in Kumasi, Ghana. He obtained his Secondary Education at Prempeh College where he passed at the top of his class. He entered Oxford University where he received his Honors BA degree in 1964 in Economics, Philosophy, and Politics, and later, a Master's degree. In 1967, he became Chief Legal Officer and City Manager of Kumasi. He was a founding member of NPP (New Patriot Party). Then in 1969, he became a Deputy Minister. He is married and has five children.

President Kufuor is a charismatic leader. He is attempting to reach the people in the rural areas in an attempt to break down social barriers. However, it is a difficult task. In a recent poll, 50% of the rural people say that they are in worse shape than this time in 2002. Only 23% of the people say that they are better off. He is using his diplomacy to mobilize and to rebuild the infrastructure of Ghana through foreign aid.

Back to Accra
Journal Entry...

When we left the carving village, we headed back to Accra. We needed to confirm our flights back for Wednesday night so we dropped our group leader and one of the tour guides off at the airlines while we traveled to the bank to make a money transfer. They caught a taxi and met us at the market. Some of the ladies wanted to return to the scene of an earlier market, the Centre for National Culture.

One lady had promised to trade some capri pants. A few others wanted to get some outfits that they had seen earlier. By now, it is about 1700 hours. We headed back to the hotel for dinner. We found out that the travel agent, again, had not scheduled for us to eat at the hotel tonight. Wednesday was our last night there and the agency would allow our last meal to be the soul food. Some one made the statement that we should be more inclined to experience foods other than what we were accustomed to.

I am not sure about the others, but after traveling for about 10 days, I just wanted to relax in the hotel the next couple of days, just have dinner, relax at the pool, and listen to the music. But tonight, we were off to the Dynasty Restaurant.

The Dynasty, as you might have imagined, is a Chinese Restaurant and Africans operate it. As we drove into the parking lot, there was a security guard standing at the entrance.

The exterior was draped with miniature white lights. As we entered the building, it also was decorated with the miniature white lights. Our seats were upstairs in a private room. All eleven of us were seated at a round table with a revolving server. The ethnic food was magnificently presented on the server. We had servings of shrimp, chicken, lamb, Red Snapper, Jollof rice, and cabbage. Dessert was a fruit dish. The food critic of the group suggested that the food was excellent and it was. We left to go back to the hotel. The professional packers were expected at 2000 hours.

Professional packers will pack up anything that will not fit in your luggage. The airport will allow passengers to check 2 pieces of luggage and carry on one piece. The 2 pieces checked can not exceed 70lbs each, otherwise you pay extra. The carry on luggage, we discovered, could not be more than about 8lbs; otherwise there was an extra charge. My group leader and one other lady had excess pieces due to the art carvings that they had purchased. The packers secured the pieces and packed them inside boxes to be shipped home. The group member who purchased the (2) 5-foot pieces was stressing because she did not know how she would get her packages from New York to North Carolina.

A couple of the ladies had outfits tailored that they were expecting that night, also. This was our last night here, and we were facing the reality that this experience was coming to an end. We retired for the evening.

Point of Interest...
Charles Ghankay Taylor

Since 1998, there had been civil unrest in Liberia, a neighboring state of Ghana. In recent months, prior to our trip, bloodshed was on the rise; needless to say the situation was getting worse. The Liberians United for Reconciliation and Democracy (LURD) was fighting to overthrow President Charles Taylor.

Charles Taylor was born in 1948, 3rd of 15 children, to a family (Americo Liberians), an elite group that grew out of the freed slaves who founded the country in the 19th century. Later, he added "Ghankay" (African name) as his middle name. He obtained an Economics degree at Bentley College in Massachusetts and returned home and obtained a job running the General Services Agency under Master Sergeant Samuel Doe who led Liberia's first successful coup in 1980.

He fell out of grace with Doe when he was accused of embezzling about $1M from the government and fled to the US. He was detained at the Massachusetts Correction Center under an extradition warrant. There were conflicting reports about his release after a year of captivity. Some say he escaped from prison by carving through the bars, others say he cut a deal to overthrow Doe's regime. He led a coup that successfully gained control of Liberia when he returned to West Africa in 1989. President Samuel Doe was murdered in the Liberian Civil War, which broke out in December 1989. His attack and killing was captured on video that was seen world-wide. Doe's ears were chopped off during the attack.

In 1997, Taylor won the presidential election. A flamboyant leader, known for extreme theatrics, he has been described as a preacher, warlord and president. So powerful, he has been seen in his car with his bodyguards running along beside him when there was a security risk. There were reports of Taylor obtaining the release of prisoners in Ghana to build his armed forces. Members of his forces included children, who dressed in costumes, wore blonde wigs, and when under the influence of drugs, were very brutal.

Now, Taylor was facing an attempt, by the LURD, to overthrow his regime. In June 2003, he was indicted in a war crime court on charges that he armed and trained rebels in Sierra Leone's Civil War in exchange for diamonds. Fifty thousand people were reported to have died during that country's 10-year war.

He had initially accepted an offer of asylum from Nigeria's President but would not say when. The LURD would not retreat until US forces stepped in. Mr. Taylor agreed to step down following the arrival of the peacekeepers. On Sunday 27-07-03, the day we arrived in Ghana, US Deputy Secretary, Paul Wolfowitz, insisted that the US forces would not move in until there was a cease-fire and Mr. Taylor left power and the country. The US pledged to send 2,000 Marines and $10M to the peacekeeping force. Ghana, Mali, Benin, Senegal, and Togo promised 3250 soldiers. On 11-08-03, Taylor did step down and accepted the Nigerian President Olusegun Obasanjo's offer. He is currently living with his wife, children, and entourage in Calabar, Nigeria.

During Liberia's 13 year unrest, more than 28,000 refugees have relocated in Ghana at Buduburam Camp about 40 km west of Accra. There were also, on record, more than 1000 refugees from Sierra Leone, We passed the camp during our travels. It is a small town with concrete houses, about 20 churches and some electricity.

Efforts by the government to make the members of the community self-sufficient have proven to be successful. There are grocery stands, communication centers, small restaurants, day care centers, and training programs for job placement. There is also a community watch organization.

I don't feel that any us in the tour group had immediate concerns for our safety, as American citizens. People that I talked with about taking the trip were concerned that the fighting would spread to Ghana as well. There was no noticeable Liberian influence in Ghana during our visit.

Day XII
Wednesday 06-08-03

Let us hear the conclusion of the whole matter;
Fear God, and keep his commandments; for this is
the whole duty of man.
For God shall bring every work into judgment,
With every secret thing, whether it be
good, or whether it be evil.
Ecclesiastes 12:13-14

Day of Reflection

Journal Entry…

    Today was a free day. We met for breakfast. Some ladies took a taxi to the fabric shop, others went back to the market. I went to the room to just sit and reflect. I took a notebook with me to journalize my daily experiences. So, I sat there reviewing my notes. I have just experienced something that I never would have imagined in a million years. I am feeling something so spiritual that I can hardly believe it. How do I expose this experience to people back home? How?

    We checked out of the hotel at 1500 hours and left our luggage in a holding area. We moved around the hotel until 1900 hours when we met for our Soul Food Dinner, finally. It was everything we expected and more.

There were collards, potato salad, several other cold salads, Paella, Jambalya, yams, ham, turkey, ribs, cabbage, and macaroni and cheese. I probably missed something but this gives you a good idea of the feast. It was wonderful! After dinner, we again hung out in the hotel until time to leave for the airport. The flight was not until 0030 hours, but we needed to report to the airport at 2200 hours.

Departure for the Airport

When we arrived at the airport, we rushed ahead of another tour group to get checked in. It's one thing to have to wait. It's another thing to have to wait standing up. Two ladies did have to pay extra for the excess weight of their luggage. One lady said she paid $50 American dollars. She did not understand how it was measured. The lady who had the two 5 foot art carvings had to pay more but did not reveal the amount. We sat until 0030 hours, boarded the plane and waited some more. We were in the air by 0130 hours. About 3 hours into the flight, we had to depart the plane for a security check in Gambia. We were told that we had to take everything with us, otherwise it would be considered suspicious.

We got off the plane, boarded a bus to the terminal. Passengers with children were allowed through first. Once there, we went through 4 checkpoints, then boarded the plane again. This took 45 minutes. When we were back on the plane, it was announced that they would be spraying a pesticide required by the US after coming from a country such as Africa.

A flight attendant went down each aisle and sprayed a mist in the air overhead. I could not really smell it and I am sensitive to the best of fragrances. But, some complained because they said they had respiratory problems and shared phone numbers and addresses with each other to compare symptoms after they arrived home. I don't seriously think anything came of that.

By now, it is about 0500 hours and a movie is played, "Maid in Manhattan" with Jennifer Lopez. We were served a continental meal, croissants, a Danish and juice. About an hour before landing, we were served a fruit cup, Danishes, and juice. The pilot, then, alerted us that we were about to land, 30 minutes ahead of schedule and the seat belt light came on. Around 1000 hours, US time, we were back on US soil. It took about 2 hours to get out of the airport, about 1 hour waiting for our luggage and another hour waiting for the oversized packages to come through. Then we were back on the streets of New York. What a joy ride I've experienced!

APPENDIX A
Regions of Ghana

Regions Of Ghana

Ten regions make of the nation of Ghana: the Upper West Region, the Upper East Region, the Northern Region, the Brong Ahafo Region, the Volta Region, the Ashanti Region, the Central Region, the Eastern Region, the Western Region, and the Greater Accra Region. The Central Region (Cape Coast), Ashanti (Kumasi) Region, and The Greater Accra (Accra) Regions have been showcased throughout the book. Although we did not travel to the other regions, this section will highlight some characteristics of those areas.

The Upper West Region

The Upper West Region is located in Northwest Ghana. **Wa** is the capital of this region. It is a rural town, population of 80,000 in 1996. Wa is a 17-hour ride from Accra on poor roads, but there is an airtaxi. Volunteers with the Peace Corp of the U.S. established a computer-training center. To qualify for computer training, you must understand the English language, know how to type and have a personal computer. Learning the computer will offer hopes of increasing job skills for higher paying jobs. There is not much demand for the Internet due to the expense of long distance connection. There are projects in place to assist the local weavers in marketing their products over the Internet.

The Upper East Region

The Upper East Region is located in Northeast Ghana. **Bolgatonga** is the capital. An HIV/AIDS Compassion Flame arrived in the Upper East Region on Wednesday 19-11-03. The flame is being taken around the country as a symbol of hope to rekindle the spirit of the Ghanaians in eradicating the disease.

A bicyclist from the Northern Region presented the flame to the Regional Minister, who in turn gave it to a farmer who will carry the torch to the Upper West Region. In an effort to reduce the stigma and discrimination of people living with HIV/AIDS, there is a call for Ghanaians to have compassion and not treat these people as outcast.

The Northern Region

The Northern Region in located in Northern Ghana. **Tamale** is the capital. Ya-na Yakubu Andani II, the 50-year-old king of Dagbon, was murdered between 25-27 March 2002. There are reports that he was beheaded, burned, and had severed limbs when found. The 2nd most powerful traditional leader in Ghana, he had been in the throne for 28 years. About 30 others were killed in the dispute between 2 royal clans, the Andanis and the Abudus. Two prime suspects were acquitted after prosecution failed to prove their case.

A state of emergency was imposed immediately after the king's death, but has recently been lifted. There is still some unrest. King Ya-na Yakubu is being preserved in a governmental hospital until a burial site is constructed. It should be completed soon and burial is expected before the end of the year.

The Brong Ahafo Region

Suyani is the capital. Women have been known to be forcibly subjected to excision in accordance with Muslim customs. Although Ghana is not an Islamic only country (15% is Muslim), the practice of clitoral excision occurs in certain parts of the North.

According to a 1994 report, a 23-year-old woman fled to Canada and claimed refugee status due to fear of persecution based on religious beliefs. She reportedly rejected the son of a prominent leader. In turn, he accused her of being promiscuous and should be persecuted. This led to her fear. It is rumored that a Catholic Priest helped her to escape.

The Volta Region

The Volta Region is located in Eastern Ghana from the Atlantic Ocean. **Ho** is the capital. The principal tribe is Ewe with about 14 dialects, including Akan. The main economic activity consist of cattle, crops, and fishing.

The cattle include sheep and goats. The crops include vegetables such as tomatoes, peppers, maize, sugar cane, and coconut. The main catches include Sardines, Anchovies, Lobster, and shrimp.

The Ashanti Region
The Ashanti Region is located in central Ghana. **Kumasi** is the capital, home of the Ashanti King, Otumfuo Osei Tutu II.

The Central Region
The central region is located on the Southern end of Ghana, bordered by the Atlantic Ocean. **Cape Coast** is the capital. Cape Coast Castle and Elmina Castle are located in this region.

The Eastern Region
The Eastern Region is located in Eastern Ghana. The area was first inhabited in 1875 by the Ashanti people. Most of the residents are traders who traveled from Akyem, Asante and Kwahu to do business there. **Koforidua** (pronounced Ko-fo-re-doo'a) is the capital. The population in 1984 was 58,731. The name for the capital was derived from a man name Kofi-Ofori who built a hut under a huge Mahogony tree. Farmers returning home at the end of a day's work on their farms would rest under the tree. In Twi, the local language for tree is *dua.* Kofi-Ofori and dua combined gives Koforidua.

The Obuotabiri Mountain offers a distinctive view here, in addition to the sun-baked tin roofs on top of the houses. At last count, there was one traffic light, a central market, a cinema hall, and several book stores. The area is also known for many Basic Schools. There is a large Catholic Church in the center of town. Also, you might get a peak at the Chief at the palace right next to the Church.

Western Region
The Western Region is located in Western Ghana. **Sekondi** (pronounced Sek'unde') is the Capital. The population in 1984 was 93,922. It is the third largest city in Ghana, an educational city with a lot of technical colleges and secondary schools. It is an industrial and commercial center of Western Ghana. An important seaport and commercial city, there is shipbuilding, railroad repairing, and cigarette industry. The city was developed around Dutch and English forts built in the 17th century.

Sekondi-Takoradi (pronounced Ta-ko-ra'de) are twin cities. SeKondi, the older of the two cities, prospered after the 1903 construction of a railroad for the mineral and timber resources. A deepwater harbor was constructed at Takoradi in 1928.

The Greater Accra Region

The Greater Accra Region is also located in Southern Ghana. **Accra** is the capital. Tema is a popular city in this region, located in SE Ghana on the Gulf of Guinea. The population in 1984 was 99,608. Since 1961, Tema has developed from a small fishing village to become a leading seaport and industrial center. Most of the country's chief export is shipped from Tema. Manufactures include aluminum, steel, soap, processed fish, chocolate, and cement.

APPENDIX B
Author's Commentary

Author's Commentary

Over the years, we have fought for our Civil Rights in the streets, in the courts, in the schools, in the restaurants, and in the shopping malls. We are still fighting for our rights. Just recently, a White sports commentator, Rush Limbaugh, disgraced the airwaves when he insulted Philadelphia Eagles quarterback, Donovan McNabb. Rush stated that McNabb, a Black quarterback, was an overrated player and the media was trying to make him appear better than he really was. It is amazing how, in the year 2003, we still have issues of race that are disgusting enough to cause a man to give up his job. The same thing happened with Trent Lott when he stated, at a party given for Strom Thurmond, that "the country would have been better off had Strom been elected President a half century earlier."

A White man once said to me, in a very comfortable state, that the college in the area of his coffee shop had lowered its standards since Blacks had enrolled. My blood started to boil as I told him about the times in high school when I opened my textbook to the names of students who did not attend that school. I told him that we got the books after the White high school (across town) finished using them. This meant that the quality of the education of Blacks was a pace behind the White students. He stood dumbfounded. I don't think that he was even aware of this fact. There have always been deficiencies in our educational system and there still are.

A recent article in News and Records, a Greensboro, NC newspaper, recapped the percentages of minorities on corporate boards in NC. Minorities comprise 28% of the state's population and 25% of the workforce. However, they hold 5.3% of board seats at the state's largest companies and in those cases, there would be no more than one per board. These numbers include white women as minorities, so the numbers for Blacks are even lower. The article stated that the boards look for diversity when selecting board members, but that includes what a candidate can bring to the table. If Blacks do not have the opportunities to achieve these higher positions to begin with, how do they get the opportunity to bring more to the table? It is difficult getting business loans from the very boards that are overlooking these Blacks. It is difficult getting contracts from the very boards that are overlooking these Blacks.

Some of the companies listed as having no minorities on their boards are:
1. Family Dollar Stores
2. INGLES Food Stores
3. Jefferson Pilot Insurance
4. Old Dominion Truck Lines
5. Piedmont Natural Gas
6. UNIFI Textiles

I would imagine some of these businesses earn half of their income from minorities. The government and big businesses need to lead the way by putting social programs in place to address these issues. History needs to accurately include the events of slavery especially in the school systems. Religion has always been a part of history. Some churches are blending cultures for worship services. We need to see more of this. To be able to worship the same God gives us a common belief.

Some Blacks favor reparation as a means for being compensated for the inhuman acts of slavery. Others feel that we need more Black representation in big business and politics. This is all good. However, I maintain that it goes even deeper than this. It took explicit sexual and drug related acting for Hallie Berry and Denzel Washington to win an Oscar. This meant that all the serious acting of Angela Bassett, Cicely Tyson, Diane Carol, and Lawrence Fishburne, just to name a few, were not representative enough for recognition as great actors. This only confirms the reality that drugs, sex, and violence are how "the powers that be" perceive Blacks in the movie business. There are not enough good examples of Blacks achieving influential positions or receiving special recognition for their accomplishments. Whether it's in the boardrooms, political positions, and even the private golf clubs, there are still problems receiving status.

Women will need greater leadership roles during the 21st century to resolve racial issues. Men, both Black and White, have become too emotional. White men, innately, still feel the need to suppress the Black man, and the Black man, innately, still feels the need to be released from bondage. Over 30 years ago, a committee of White men shut down the Black high school in the community where I lived. Just recently, a committee of influential White women, understanding the impact of this educational landmark in the early 1900's, obtained financing to remodel and reopen the school (within the Guilford County School System) as the Penn Griffin School of the Arts in High Point, NC.

My charge to my Brothers and my Sisters—" go see the Motherland." Allow yourselves the opportunity to experience what I have. I feel this trip did for me what Malcolm X's visit to Mecca did for him. I came back with a new perspective on life. There is a saying that you can not know where you are going until you know where you have been. Until you walk the floors of those slave dungeons, you do not know where you have been. Until you see the gutters carved in the floor to drain away urine and feces, you do not know where you have been. Until you see the "Slave River" where the Slaves took their last bath before being auctioned, I submit to you that you do not know where you have been.

If you have a way to lend services or skills to improve life there, do so. To all others, the facts of history are immutable. Until these facts are accepted as the cause of racial disharmony and accurately recorded as a part of history, we all will continue to be haunted for generations to come, either through disenfranchisement of rights or we will face continuous conquests for those rights.

To the people, I dedicate this poem:

Unless

Unless our men are wearing baggy pants and dealing drugs,
Unless our women are exposing back creases to the camera,
Unless our children excel in Ebonics,
Unless our men increase jail time,
5   Unless our single female parent households are increasing,
Unless our children's academic scores are decreasing,
Unless our men are producing gangster rap,
Unless our women are portraying subservient roles,
Unless our children are born on crack,
10   Unless our men are unemployed,
Unless our women are on welfare,
Unless our children are abandoned,
We never get the exposure or recognition due.
Blacks have struggled and continue to struggle
15   Because of the need for society to differentiate;
From the Mayflower to the Twin Towers,
From the lunch counters to the retail counters,
From the bus seats to the theatre seats,
From the neighboring schools to quotas for school,
20   From the rights to vote to voting right,
From job equity to equal pay,
From the rest room to the board room,
From class action to Affirmative Action,
From the Supreme Court to major sports,
25   From racial woes to political roles,
Blacks have struggled and continue to struggle
Until we as a society, collectively identify the real problems
And then collectively work to improve life for all.
It is imperative that we do so, **Unless** we choose to collectively
30   perish as a nation.

APPENDIX C
Recipes of West African Dishes

Recipes Of West African Dishes

The following recipes are representative of some of the dishes that we experienced while in Africa. There is a special cornbread recipe offered by my mother, Eloise.

African Fruit Salad

1	Lb	Papaya
2		Mangos-1 Lb. Each
1	Large	Pineapple-3-4 lb
2	Large	Bananas

We were served a fruit salad as dessert most nights. Select bananas that have just turned ripe. You can make the salad up to 4 hrs ahead of time, then cover with plastic wrap and refrigerate. Add the bananas just before serving, however, or they will turn brown. The fruits must be all cut into very small pieces for the dish to be at its best.

Peel the Papayas, cut in half and scoop out the seeds. Continue to cut the halves into small pieces and place into a large bowl. Peel the Mangos and follow the same process as with the Papaya.

Using a sturdy, sharp knife, cut the top and bottom off of the pineapple. Set the Pineapple upright on a cutting board. Working from the top to the bottom, slice off the dark, prickly outside skin. Cut the Pineapple lengthwise into quarters, then again to remove the tough inner core on each quarter. Cut the quarters into small pieces, retain all juices. Add the pineapple and juices to the other fruits. Toss well, cover and refrigerate until well chilled. Just before serving, peel the bananas and cut into small pieces. Add to the bowl, toss well and serve. Yield: 8 servings.

AFRICAN SQUASH AND YAMS (FUTARI)

1	Small	Onion-chopped
2	Tb	Oil
1	Lb	Hubbard Squash-pared and cut into 1-inch pieces
2	Medium	Yams or Sweet Potatoes-pared and cut into 1-inch pieces
1	Cup	Coconut Milk
½	Ts	Salt
½	Ts	Ground Cinnamon
1/3	Ts	Ground Cloves

Cook and stir onion in oil in 10-inch skillet over medium heat until tender. Stir in remaining ingredients. Heat to boiling. Reduce heat. Cover and simmer 10 minutes. Simmer, uncovered, stirring occasionally, until vegetables are tender, about 5 minutes longer. Yield: 6 to 8 servings

Avocado Stuffed with Smoked Fish

4		Hard-cooked Eggs*
¼	Cup	Milk
¼	Cup	Strained Fresh Lime Juice
¼	Ts	Sugar
½	Ts	Salt
1/3	Cup	Vegetable Oil
2	Tb	Olive Oil
½	Lb	Smoked Whitefish
2	Large	Ripe Avocados
12	Strips	Fresh Red Bell Pepper or canned Pimiento**

* The yolks rubbed through a sieve and the whites finely chopped
** Each cut about ¼ inch wide and 2 inches long

In a mixing bowl, mash the egg yolks and milk together with a fork until they form a smooth paste. Add 1 tablespoon of the lime juice, the sugar and the salt.

Then mix the vegetable oil, a teaspoon at a time; make sure each addition is absorbed before adding more. Add the olive oil by teaspoonfuls, beating constantly. Stir the remaining lime juice into the sauce and taste for seasoning. Using a small knife, remove the skin from the fish and pick out any bones. Drop the fish into a bowl and flake it finely with a fork. Add the chopped egg whites and the sauce, and toss together gently but thoroughly.

Just before serving, cut the avocados in half. With the tip of a small knife, loosen the seeds and lift them out. Remove any brown tissue like fibers clinging to the flesh. Spoon the fish mixture into the avocado halves, dividing it equally among them and mounding it slightly in the center. Arrange 3 strips of sweet pepper or pimiento diagonally across the top of each avocado and serve at once. Yield: 4 servings.

Avocado with Groundnut Dressing

2		Avocados-Ripe
1	Tb	Lemon Juice
2	Tb	Peanuts-Shelled
½	Ts	Paprika
½	Ts	Cinnamon
		Cayenne Pepper-to Taste
		Salt-to Taste
		Fresh Chives-to Garnish

Peel the avocados and cut into cubes. Sprinkle with lemon juice and set aside. Grind the peanuts roughly in a grinder for a few seconds. Mix the peanuts and spices well. Sprinkle over the avocados with finely chopped chives. Refrigerate until ready to serve.

FRIED CABBAGE

1	Small	Onion, finely chopped
6	Tb	Oil
1	Large	Tomato, sliced
½	Ts	Salt
½	Ts	Curry Powder
1	Medium	Cabbage, shredded
2		Carrots, sliced into rounds
½	Cup	Water
1		Green Bell Pepper, Chopped

Preheat the oil on medium heat and add the onion. Cook until lightly browned. Add tomatoes, salt, and curry powder. Continue to saute' for 3 minutes. Add cabbage, carrots, and pepper, mix well. Pour in about ½ cup water. Cover the pot, reduce heat and simmer until the liquid is absorbed and the cabbage is still slightly crunchy.

JOLLOF RICE (WEST AFRICAN PAELLA)

1		Chicken (preferably fillet)
6	Medium	Onions, Chopped
6		Green Bell Peppers, Chopped
½	Lb	Shrimp
¾	Cup	Carrots, Chopped
¾	Cup	Stringbeans, broken into pieces
¾	Cup	Peas
6		Tomatoes, Chopped
1	Ts	Salt
½	Ts	Fresh Ground Pepper
1	Sprig	Thyme, crushed or 1 Ts dried Thyme
4	Cups	Rice
¼	Cup	Tomato Paste
		Oil for Frying
1 ½	Lb	Cayenne Pepper

You may use as many kinds of meat or vegetables as you wish. Use a heavy skillet to avoid burning. Using a large wooden spoon, stir often to avoid sticking. Cover the pot tightly. Cut the chicken into 1-inch square pieces.

Using a skillet large enough to hold all ingredients, brown the chicken in oil. Add onions and peppers. Cook over medium heat for 5 to 10 minutes. Saute' the shrimp in a small amount of oil in another skillet. Partially cook all the vegetables except the tomatoes, then drain. Add to the chicken skillet along with the shrimp, tomatoes, salt, pepper and thyme. Lower the heat and cook for an additional 5 minutes.

Combine rice with just enough tomato paste to give it an orange tint. Stir the coated rice into the main skillet. Allowing to simmer, add water sparingly, and stir to avoid burning. When the meat, vegetables, and rice are tender, the Paella is ready to serve.

WEST AFRICAN CHICKEN AND GROUNDNUT STEW

2	Whole	Boneless-Skinless Chicken Breasts, cut into ½ inch pieces
1	Tb	Peanut Oil
1	Medium	Onion, Chopped
1		Garlic Clove, Minced
28	Oz	Can Whole Tomatoes, undrained, cut up
15 ½	Oz	Can Green Giant Great Northern Beans, undrained
11	Oz	Can Green Giant Niblets Golden Sweet Corn, drained
1		Sweet Potato, peeled and chopped
¾	Cup	Water
¼	Cup	Peanut Butter
1	Tb	Tomato Paste
1	Ts	Salt
1	Ts	Chili Powder
½	Ts	Ginger
½	Ts	Cayenne Pepper
3	Cups	Hot Cooked Rice

In a 4-quart Dutch oven over medium-high heat, cook chicken in oil until chicken is lightly browned and no longer pink, stirring frequently. Add onion and garlic; cook and stir 3 to 4 minutes or until onion is tender. Add remaining ingredients except rice; mix well. Bring to a boil.

Reduce heat to medium-low, cover and cook 30 minutes or until sweet potato is tender, stirring occasionally. If stew becomes too thick, add additional water. Serve stew over hot rice. Yield: 8 servings

Red Snapper

5	Lbs	Snapper
		Salt and Pepper-to Taste
½		Lime
¼	Cup	Flour
1	Cup	Rice
1	Cup	Chopped Raw Shrimp
½	Cup	Chopped Green Onions, including tops
½	Cup	Very Thinly Sliced Celery
1	Tb	Grated Ginger Root
2	Slices	Bacon
¼	Cup	Dry White Wine

Season red snapper with salt and pepper, inside and out. Rub with the lime. Sprinkle evenly with the flour. Combine rice, shrimp, onion, celery, and ginger root. Spoon into fish. Skewer and sew opening. Lay fish in a heavily buttered baking pan. Score the top of the fish in an attractive design to prevent the fish from buckling. Lay bacon slices over the top. Bake at 350 degrees for 45 minutes or until fish flakes. Transfer fish to a warm platter. De-glaze baking pan with white dry wine. Pour liquid over fish.

Eloise's Cornbread (My Mother's Cornbread)

2	Boxes	Jiffy Cornbread Mix
1/3	Cup	Self-rising Flour
3		Eggs
2	Sticks	Margarine
1	Tb	Krisco Oil
1	Cup	Dairy Milk

Grease baking pan with Krisco oil. Preheat oven at 350. Combine cornbread mix, flour, eggs, and milk in a large bowl. Melt butter and stir into mix quickly. Pour mixture into baking pan and place pan into the oven. Bake about 20 minutes or until golden brown. Brush the top with a little margarine. Yield: 10-12

This cornbread recipe will make the meal complete.

APPENDIX D
Guide to Ghana

Guide To Ghana

Passport
If you have not already done so, you will need to apply for a passport. You can do this through you local postal service. There is a 4-6 week turn around on delivery. If you use one of the walk-in centers, you will need to schedule an appointment. These centers serve customers who are traveling within 2 weeks (14 days) or who need a foreign visa. If you should have to use one of the walk-in centers, plan on staying 4-6 hours. The passport application requires 2 photos. The photos can be taken and purchased for an additional cost at the post office, some copy centers, and pharmacies.

Visa
You will need a visa that is required to enter the country. You will receive an application to obtain a visa. The application will probably state that you will receive your visa in about 5 days. In reality, it may take considerably longer than 5 days. Plan accordingly.

Vaccinations
I used the International Travel Center at the local health department. Your family physician may be able to administer the medication and give you additional suggestions about the inoculations. You will be given a record of your shots. Keep this record with your passport.

Yellow Fever

A Yellow Fever vaccination is required. Yellow fever is a disease that occurs in many countries in Africa and South America. The disease is transmitted to humans by mosquitoes. This is administered through an injection. Travelers must take the injection at least 10 days before entry into the country.

Meningococcal Meningitis

Meningococcal Meningitis injections are optional. People can acquire the disease by inhaling the bacteria (when an infected person coughs on them), by direct mouth-to-mouth contact with an infected person.

Hepatitis A

Protection from Hepatitis A is optional. Poor personal hygiene, poor sanitation, and intimate contact are all factors that allow for transmission of the virus, which are shed in the feces of infected persons. Most of the people acquire the disease by drinking fecally-contaminated water, or by eating contaminated food.

Hepatitis B

Protection from Hepatitis B is optional. Hepatitis B is an infection of the liver caused by the Hepatitis B virus (HBV). HBV is passed from one person to another in blood or certain body secretions (including wound-clotting fluids, semen, vaginal discharge, saliva, tears and urine). People can acquire the disease during sexual relations or when sharing things such as toothbrushes, razors, or needles used to inject drugs. Those people infected with HBV who become chronic carriers can spread the infection to others throughout their lifetime. They can also develop long-term liver disease such as cirrhosis (which destroys the liver) or liver cancer.

Malaria

Malaria remains the most important infectious disease and most frequent infectious cause of death for persons traveling to countries in the tropics and subtropics. Even if your stay is brief such as a 1-night stay in a malarious area, you should take protective measures. Malaria is an infection caused by a single-celled blood parasite that is transmitted through the bite of the Anopheles mosquito.

It occurs in many parts of the world, including Central and South America, Africa, the Indian subcontinent, Southeast Asia, the Middle East, and islands of the South Pacific. The risk of malaria is highest between dusk and dawn, the time that Anopheles mosquitoes feed on humans. Malarone, Aralen, Lariam, and Doxycycline are the primary drugs. Dosage and instructions on use may vary.

Luggage

You will want to purchase protection insurance in the event the trip is canceled. Carry a few bottles of water until you can purchase extra. Purchase canned items such as tuna, fruit cups, juices and other canned meats. You will also want to purchase crackers, cookies, and dried fruit. Purchase a sunblock, #45 is good, and an insect repellant. Purchase headache pills and antacids. You will also need to take a 220 adapter for your small electrical appliances.

You will want to pack clothing and other items that you maybe able to barter for African clothes and art. Unloading these items will leave room for your newly purchased items on the return trip. A tip for packing: roll your items before you place them in your suitcase. This allows room for more items. Pack casual wear, such as shorts, capris, pants, and tops. You will need a pair of casual walking shoes, preferably tennis shoes. A light jacket is necessary for the cool evenings. A hat will also be needed. You will also want to purchase a fannie-pack or some type of item you can wear on your waist or under your clothes to hold you money and personal items. You will need to keep your passport on you at all times.

The flight will be a minimum of 11 hours. An overnight flight will make it easier to rest and prepare for the time change (4 hours ahead of Eastern Standard Time). It would be wise to have a back or neck pillow to help keep you comfortable during the trip. You will have an opportunity to move around once you receive permission from the flight captain.

**For Additional questions about the trip or tours, e-mail
daysofghana@yahoo.com**

APPENDIX E
Words to Remember

Words To Remember

Accra (pronounced Ah'-cra) Capital of Ghana

Adinkra (pronounced a-din-kra) Ashanti term, African symbols used in clothing and art design.

Agoo' (pronounced ah-goo) May I have your attention?

Ahwiaa - Wood Carving Village

Akwaaka (pronounced ah-wa-ka) welcome

Akwankwaa - young man

Amee' (pronounced ah-may) Yes

Annafi Forex Bureau- facility to exchange money.

Ashantehene - King of Ashante

Ashanti - term used for the Ashante people during pre-independence times.

Beento's (been to's) those who have been to another land and returned.

Bonwire (pronounced Bon-wi'-re) home of Kente Village.

Cedi- (pronounced cd) Ghanaian money

Diaspora- (pronounced Di-as'-po-ra) Blacks, outside of Africa, scattered around the world.

Elmina (pronounced El-me-na) town in Central Region of Ghana, home of Elmina Castle.

Eyie- Adinkra cloth which means farewell.

Kente cloth (pronounced Ken-te')- woven material, indigenous to country of Ghana.

Kradin - Soul Name, based on day child was born is the day the child's soul decided to come forth onto the world.

NEPAD- New Partnership for Africa's Development

Ntoma - factory made cloth similar to Kente cloth.

Ntomso - home of the Adinkra Cloth.

PANAFEST- Pan African Festival

Scheme - Ghanaian reference for contribution or project to promote improvements.

TroTro-Bus

APPENDIX F

Metric Table Measurements

Metric Table Measurements

Ghana uses the Metric System. So for you convenience, I have included some measurements for your familiarity.

Kilometer- metric unit of distance equal to 3280.8 ft or 621 statute miles.

1000 grams	= 1kg
100,000 centigrams	= 1kg
1,000,000 milligrams	= 1kg
1000 milligrams	= 1 gram
1000 kilograms	= 1 metric ton
1000 millimeters	= 1 meter
100 centimeters	= 1 meter
1000 meters	= 1 kilometer
0.035 ounces	= 1 gram
2.2046 pounds	= 1 Kilogram
1 ounce	= 28.35 grams
1 pound	= 0.45359 Kilograms

Multiply inches by 2.54 to get centimeters
Multiply feet by 0.305 to get meters

Multiply miles by 1.6 to get kilometers
Divide pounds by 2.2 to get kilograms
Multiply ounces by 28 to get grams
Multiply fluid ounces by 30 to get milliliters
Multiply gallons by 3.8 to get liters

1 inch	= 25.4 millimeters
1 pound	= 453.59237 grams
1 gallon	= 3.785411784 liters
1 milliliter	= 1 cubic centimeter

Temperature is expressed in degrees Celcius in the metric system. Celcius- the boiling point at sea level is 100°Celcius or 100°C. Freezing at sea level is 0°C. 86°F is equal to 30°C.

APPENDIX G

Military Time Schedule

Military Time Schedule

Your travel information from Ghana maybe recorded in military time. The following is a schedule of military time.

0000 hours	midnight	1200 hours	12:00pm
0100 hours	1:00am	1300 hours	1:00pm
0200 hours	2:00am	1400 hours	2:00pm
0300 hours	3:00am	1500 hours	3:00pm
0400 hours	4:00am	1600 hours	4:00pm
0500 hours	5:00am	1700 hours	5:00pm
0600 hours	6:00am	1800 hours	6:00pm
0700 hours	7:00am	1900 hours	7:00pm
0800 hours	8:00am	2000 hours	8:00pm
0900 hours	9:00am	2100 hours	9:00pm
1000 hours	10:00am	2200 hours	10:00pm
1100 hours	11:00am	2300 hours	11:00pm

The dates are recorded day, month, year, example 30-09-71 is 30th day, September 1971.

APPENDIX H
Cedi Exchange Rate

Us Dollars   **Cedi**   **Exchange**   **Rate**

Year 2003

Us Dollars	Cedi
1.00	8,600.00
5.00	43,000.00
10.00	86,000.00
50.00	430,000.00
100.00	860,000.00
200.00	1,720,000.00

Previous exchange rates: Cedis per US Dollar

6895.77 (January 2001)
5321.68 (2000)
2647.32 (1999)
2314.15 (1998)
2050.17 (1997)
1637.23 (1996)

APPENDIX I
Bibliography

Bibliography

HYPERLINK http://www.africaonline.com
HYPERLINK http//www.allafrica.com
HYPERLINK http://www.ask.elibrary.com
HYPERLINK http://www.bbc.co.uk
HYPERLINK http://www.cnn.com/2003/world/africa/06/10/liberia.taylor
HYPERLINK http://www.crisismagazine.com
HYPERLINK http://www.dfid.gov.uk
HYPERLINK http://www.empirezine.com
HYPERLINK http://www.ghana.co.ul.news
HYPERLINK http://www.ghana.com.uk
HYPERLINK http://www.ghanaweb.com
HYPERLINK http://www.marshall.edu/akanart/cloth
HYPERLINK http://www.thp.org/prize/93/rawlings.htm
HYPERLINK http://www.recipesource.com
HYPERLINK http://www.welltempered.net

- Fred Agbeyegbe, "Ajo Productions" presents Human Cargo,   (July 2003).
- "Daily Graphic," Taylor Accepts US Plan, (August 2003), 5.
- Emancipation Pilgrimage to the Motherland Publication, (July 2003).
- "GNA News,"(July 2003).
- Land Tours Ghana Limited: Publication, (July 2003).

- Dr. Arthur King, "News and Records," <u>Companies Seek Balance On Corporation Executive Boards,</u> (September 2003), A8.
- Daniel Agbeyebiawo, <u>The life and Works of W.E.B. Du Bois,</u> (1999).

About The Author

Dot Henderson was born in Spartanburg, SC and raised in High Point, NC. She attended Virginia Union University in Richmond, VA and completed a degree in Business Education at North Carolina A&T State University in Greensboro, NC.

Made in the USA
Lexington, KY
28 November 2011